Praise for *Broken Heart, Shared Heart, Healing Heart*

"With contemporary stories, historical facts and examples, psychological and sociological research, and even etymologies, *Broken Heart, Shared Heart, Healing Heart* reaches across time and place to assure us that for as long as humans have lived with animals, we've felt their loss as a potent grief. And it offers what we've learned about living well with their loss. This book builds a camaraderie of wounded, healing hearts."

—**Gayle Boss**, author of *All Creation Waits* and *Wild Hope*

"If you've experienced the love and loss of a treasured nonhuman companion, this gem of a book is for you. Filled with wisdom and compassion, it is a true salve for the grieving heart."

—**Leah Kaminsky**, physician and author of ten books, including *Doll's Eye*

"Barbara Allen's time as an animal chaplain has given her incredible insight into pet loss and how profound grief can surround the loss of a furry family member. With great love comes great grief, and Allen gives excellent insight into the human-animal bond. We don't discuss grief and death enough as a Western society, and this book gives examples of how other cultures handle the death of a beloved pet and ways we can cope with this profound loss. Pet parents and people in the veterinary field will benefit from reading this comforting and well-written book."

—**Kaitlin Howard**, MSSW, certified pet loss coach at Lap of Love Veterinary Hospice

"Losing a pet is heartbreaking. *Broken Heart, Shared Heart, Healing Heart* by Barbara Allen is a beautiful book that recognizes the loss of a pet and offers comfort and guidance by exploring how people process grief, different ways you can honor your pet, and how some religions view the death of a pet. I highly recommend this special book that will bring comfort to those grieving their pet."

—**Joanna Rowland**, author of *The Memory Box: A Book about Grief*

Broken Heart, Shared Heart, Healing Heart

Broken Heart, Shared Heart, Healing Heart

Navigating the Loss of Your Pet

BARBARA ALLEN

Broadleaf Books
Minneapolis

BROKEN HEART, SHARED HEART, HEALING HEART
Navigating the Loss of Your Pet

Library of Congress Cataloging-in-Publication Data

Names: Allen, Barbara (Ordained minister), author.
Title: Broken heart, shared heart, healing heart : navigating the loss of
   your pet / Barbara Allen.
Description: Minneapolis : Broadleaf Books, [2024] | Includes
   bibliographical references.
Identifiers: LCCN 2023039834 (print) | LCCN 2023039835 (ebook) | ISBN
   9781506493565 (hardback) | ISBN 9781506493572 (ebook)
Subjects: LCSH: Grief--Psychological aspects. | Pets--Death--Psychological
   aspects. | Pet owners--Psychology.
Classification: LCC BF575.G7 A543 2024 (print) | LCC BF575.G7 (ebook) |
   DDC 155.9/37--dc23/eng/20231201
LC record available at https://lccn.loc.gov/2023039834
LC ebook record available at https://lccn.loc.gov/2023039835

Cover design: Jamison Spittler
Cover image: shutterstock_330716366.eps/shutterstock_360094553.eps/shutterstock_608818742.eps/shutterstock_762314248.eps/shutterstock_1150239107.eps

Print ISBN: 978-1-5064-9356-5
eBook ISBN: 978-1-5064-9357-2

Printed in China

For my husband, David, my soul mate of forty years, who died during the writing of this book. Thank you for your encouragement, and for your deep, deep love. You are now spirit walking with Honey, Lucy, Rosa, and Primo.

For Rhys, Di, Bernadette, Harry, and Leaf.

For my former clients, who allowed me to accompany them through times of overwhelming sorrow; you and your animal companions taught me so much. You are such good, good, compassionate people; I hope your hearts have healed a little.

And to God, Creator of all. Thank you for blessing us with feathered, furred, and finned brethren.

CONTENTS

INTRODUCTION

I RECENTLY PICKED up a book in my local library. The book had nothing to do with animals; it was a fantasy novel for young adults. The book fell open to the dedication page, where I read: "to the dogs who have gone ahead on the longest of all walks."

Much of my time spent musing over the outline of this book took place while walking my middle-aged, blind rescue dog, Harry. One of our special spots is a large park. An oasis of green, it borders a university and several large hospitals. My favorite bench honors the life of a scholar and actor who loved walking in the park with his dogs. The wooden seat is marked by a plaque with this heartfelt inscription: "Now they walk in the High Garden. Everyone comes, nobody goes. It's wonderful."

I ponder these words as I remember not only my own pets who have died but also the hundreds I met during my time as a chaplain at an animal hospital. I have spent many years providing people with support as they grieve for a beloved animal companion. I have been a chaplain at the Lort Smith Animal Hospital, in Melbourne, Australia, the largest animal hospital in the Southern Hemisphere. Most of my work was helping clients before, during, and after their much-loved pet was euthanized, had died during surgery, or had been diagnosed with a life-threatening illness. Every year, I spoke to over fifteen hundred clients.

It was precious work, a privilege, to meet clients' pets, comfort the grieving, and listen to stories about their beautiful animal companions.

Every evening I would return home feeling richer than when I had left that morning.

Personally, I have been fortunate to have always had animal companions as part of my family. Indeed I cannot remember *not* having an animal companion. My time in ministry at Lort Smith meant I acquired a number of animal companions (they also operated a rescue shelter). These rescued animal companions taught me valuable lessons.

Not long after I started chaplaincy there, I acquired my first addition. She was a heavily pregnant fox terrier mix, found tied up outside the hospital gates by a lead fashioned from a string of rosary beads. I named her Rosa, after the rosary beads. My righteous anger at the people who had tortured her with cigarettes (burns were on her neck) and shot her (pellets were in her legs) was softened by the fact that at least someone had done the right thing by bringing her—pregnant and ravenous—to a safe haven. Rosa loved all humans, all dogs, all cats. She did not hold grudges. She had forgiven humans.

My cat, Pigeon, was rescued by a driver who saw her thrown from a moving vehicle. She too possessed the sweetest nature. All were welcomed into her presence. She was my vibrating Zen cat, always purring, never a scratch or protest from her.

We have stories of how we found (or were found by) our animal companions. What lessons did they teach us? Do we still observe or honor those important lessons?

Sometimes one of the most important lessons is that of accepting our mortality, and the mortality of all other beings, especially those whom we love.

Back in the park, as Harry and I sit in the cool, hardly warmed by the rays of the winter sun, I feel enveloped by a lightness of spirit. We sit. I watch. Harry listens and smells. Elderly walkers trundle by, often accompanied by slow, arthritic dogs. Young, energetic people sprint past, paced by fast dogs or slowed by ones taking their time, sniffing, rolling, knowing their owner will eventually look back . . . stop . . . and wait.

What do they have in common? Hearts. Pets. Hearts for each other. Relationships bonded, held fast, by love.

From a Christian or Jewish perspective, the God-given privilege bestowed upon Adam of "naming" the animals in the garden might contribute to the bond as well. To name is relational, at times a sacred activity or a vow. We may feel closer to someone, human or nonhuman, if we know their names or have named them.

Companion animals provide support, love, and loyalty. They have their own roles within a family or with their carer. When they die, they are missed. The ending of this physical relationship can be one of the most difficult times in a person's life, made even more difficult by our living in a society that often denies the pain and process of death. This book deals with the pain of pet loss, a grief that is now better understood than it was in the past, but I still think it has some way to go.

Humans across all cultures have been trying to make sense of grief and death since the beginning of time. In a First Peoples' myth of the Shoshoni people of the Western Plains, death came about due to a trick. Coyote didn't want to bring the dead back to life because there would be too many people and not enough resources. Wolf agreed, but he decided that Coyote's son would be the first to die. Of course, Coyote regretted his words, but it was too late. Death had entered the world and was staying.

Other Indigenous peoples' myths say death is brought into the world by animals, but so too is grief, its accompanying shadow. In one tale, Coyote bequeaths humans the experience of grief after the death of his daughter. As Coyote weeps, he says: "This sorrow I feel is great.

From this day forward, I will pass on these feelings to humans, and when they lose a loved one, they, too, will know the sorrow of Coyote."

If you are reading this book, you likely know that sorrow as you are grieving—or anticipating—the loss of a beloved pet or as you are helping a family member or friend through the pain of pet loss. If you are grieving, please accept my condolences. If you are reading this to help someone, thank you for caring.

It is important to remember that the category "pets" is broader than the inclusion of only cats and dogs. There are birds, fish, rats, horses, guinea pigs, hamsters, and rabbits. Some clients have pet snakes and lizards. The bond between species is strong. Even if we are unfamiliar with what life might be like with a rabbit, or a hamster, or a fish, we must be careful that our lack of knowledge, our ignorance, does not became a tool of judgment. Here is a moving account from a client of mine about his love of and for rabbits, and how deep his bond is:

> *I picked her up out of her cage and held her against my breast, her feet trembling, and we looked into each other's eyes. With funny whiskers sprouting out of eyebrows, nose and cheeks, floppy ears . . . I knew she was the one. . . . My dear Meg has gone but she will live with me always in my heart and will only die when I cease to remember her. . . . I have buried Meg next to Coffee near the back fence that looks over the Barwon River as they have company in eternity with each other and their spirits can run free. It also allows me to look over to their graves and remember them each day when I am outside sitting in my chair.*

Tears still gather in my eyes when I reread this section of the three-page handwritten letter. The client concluded his correspondence by adding that this was the first letter that he had written in about thirty years. What does that do for our understanding concerning the bond, the grief, and the depths of love?

We grieve because we love. If we didn't love, we wouldn't grieve. This doesn't make death any easier. Our hearts break when our animal companions die.

We should never have to justify that we grieve for an animal companion. They were part of our families, our friends, and therefore entitled to respect. When they die, we are allowed to grieve. Most animals have shorter life spans than humans, but they live forever in our hearts. Because of this, throughout this book, I have used the symbol of the heart as a thread and link between chapters. Between each chapter is a section called a Heartbeat, which tells the story of a famous person and their beloved animal companion.

With the exception of jellyfish and similar creatures, all animals have hearts. Human hearts consist of four chambers: two ventricles and two atria. Other animal hearts are a little different: octopus and squid have three hearts, frogs have one heart with three chambers, fish have two chambers in their hearts, and, in case you were wondering, cockroaches have thirteen heart chambers! Our hearts connect us to our animal friends.

I thought of this this week as I tidied up the ornaments and mementos that vie for space on my mantelpiece. This was not a quick or easy process because I am very much a "clutter bug" or a "magpie of memories," holding on to items that garner meaning for me. I picked up a thank-you card given to me following a session I conducted about pet loss. It was black and white, with small drawings of dogs and paw prints within a large, stylized heart. What I hadn't realized until that moment was that the border of the heart was actually a leash. Both ends of the leash met at the bottom of the heart, at its point, where the handle of the leash intersected with its buckle. The leash seemed to hold the heart together, combining touch and smell, scent of dog, stroke of human.

Hearts. Our hearts, our animal companions' hearts, connected.

The Hebrew word for dog is *kelev*: כלב. The word consists of *ke*, meaning "like," and *lev*, meaning "heart." So in Hebrew, dog means "like (or as) a heart." The word may also be related to *kol* or "all," which would mean "with the whole heart." The word for puppy is even more astounding: *k'luvluv*, which sounds similar to the "lub-dub" of a heartbeat.

In case you haven't had enough of a Hebrew lesson, the last letter in dog is ב. This letter is *beth*, which can mean "house" or "dwelling place."

No matter the exact meaning, our dogs endear themselves to our hearts. Our dogs (indeed all our companion animals) live within our hearts. Whether in the flesh or in spirit, they dwell within us, always.

A note here as we begin: There is some discussion about whether we should call our animal family "pets" or "animal companions" or "animal guardians." Some individuals and animal rights groups dislike the term "pet" because they say it implies ownership, and that the animal is regarded as a possession. That is one interpretation, but don't we sometimes call our human family and friends similar names, such as "Honey" or "Cutie-pie," even "Pet"? In the end, using the term "pet" is fine if used as a term of endearment, according both human and nonhuman dignity and respect, yet being mindful of its negative subtext. I quite like the phrase "animal companion," because "companion" comes from the Latin *com* and *panis*, meaning "eating bread (or food) together." Throughout this book I will use both terms.

HEARTBEAT

YOU CAN NEVER be too old to have your first animal companion. Sigmund Freud didn't have a dog until he was nearly seventy years old. His daughter Anna had acquired a German shepherd, whom she named Wolf, and Freud was smitten. Then in 1928, he was given a chow, named Lun Yu, by a friend. Freud loved Lun Yu deeply, but sadly fifteen months later, Lun Yu was killed in an accident. After mourning for some months, Freud was given another chow, the sister of Lun Yu, named Jofi (some write "Yofi"). Dogs helped Freud deal with difficult events in his own life, such as birthdays, which he hated to celebrate. Anna made her father's birthday quite an occasion, having the dogs (Jofi, and her two dogs, Wolf and Tattoun) write a poem. The poem would be attached to one of their collars, and paraded in to be presented to the delighted Sigmund. Freud, with great ceremony, would read out the poem. The dogs would sit at the table, and both dogs and humans would be fitted out in party hats. If the poem had been attributed to a particular dog, then that dog would have the first slice of birthday cake.

Jofi was one of the first dogs to be recognized as having worked as a therapy animal. Freud's consulting room was in his house and, over time, Freud had Jofi sit in attendance during his psychotherapy sessions. Freud thought that dogs had a calming influence on people, and that they could read emotional states. It was noted that Jofi would lie near a calm patient but keep her distance from an anxious client. Jofi seemed to know when a session was due to conclude, because after fifty minutes or so, she would stretch, then go over to the door. Freud said he never needed a watch, because Jofi knew when the hour was up.

For the next seven years, Jofi was Freud's inseparable companion. Jofi was of great comfort to Freud when he underwent several operations for mouth cancer. In January 1937, Jofi had her own surgery. She died several days later from heart failure. Heartbroken, Freud wrote to German novelist Arnold Zweig: "Apart from any mourning, it is very unreal, and one wonders when one will get used to it. But, of course, one cannot easily get over seven years of intimacy."

I

SHATTERED HEARTS

Feelings in the Wake of Pet Loss

WHEN AN ANIMAL companion dies, the ratio of grief is not dependent upon the species but upon the love, the bond. The species is different, but *difference* does not mean *dilution*. When a much-loved pet dies, the grief you may feel can be overwhelming. What I want to state from the outset is this: what you are feeling is normal, and you are not being overly sentimental. When I was speaking with clients, many would hesitate, before apologizing for not being able to get words out or for crying, for tears. Sometimes this unease was accompanied by sentences such as, "My friends say it was only a dog [cat, fish, bird . . .]. It wasn't a human." Or, laden with guilt, they would cart out the emotional scales, saying something judgmental along the lines of, "I don't know what's wrong with me. I can't stop crying over the loss of my dog, but I didn't cry like this when my father died. There must be something wrong with me." Sometimes a statement like that was accompanied by tragic, self-damning words: "I must be an awful person."

Why? Because you seem to have shed more tears for your animal companion, who was with you 24/7 and loved you unconditionally? People who feel guilty over this weigh grief on both sides of the scales. We grieve because we love. We don't have a set amount of grief allocated for our loved ones. We talk about love, saying there is always enough love to go around and that we can never run out of love. The same is true about grief. There is always enough grief to be drawn on if we have loved; they go hand in hand. When we grieve, we miss the subject of our love, human and nonhuman.

Normalizing Grief

Someone once said, "Having a dog will bless you with many of the happiest days of your life, and one of the worst days." And indeed, when we lose our pet, our grief is deep—lasting far beyond one terrible day.

Grief is a normal reaction to loss, and to change. It is also a process when we realize that things will never be as they were; life will never be the same again. In the introduction, I shared the story about death's presence brought into being by Coyote's rash words. Coyote pined for his son, who became the first creature to experience the permanency of death. In another story, Coyote bestows on us the gift of grief: the deep suffering Coyote felt after his daughter's death, we now feel when a loved one has died. Poor Coyote! Of course, we do not hold Coyote responsible for the reality of death or for the heartache of grief, but from our own experiences, and those of others, we know that these two are partners, the best of friends. They travel together, share beds, and have their destinies forever entwined.

We love our animals. Recent surveys confirm this. In a 2021–22 survey, 70 percent of US households (90.5 million families) reported owning a pet. When the same industry group did their first survey in

1988, the percentage was 56 percent. In Australia, where I live, there is high pet ownership, with at least 60 percent of households having at least one pet, with over twenty-nine million pets Australia-wide (there are more pets than people; Australia's population is twenty-five million). In the UK, the percentage was quite a bit lower, until COVID-19. In 2022, UK pet ownership had risen to 62 percent, a sharp rise from its 2011–12 and 2019–20 percentages, which hovered at around 45 percent.

Because of our societal and personal love of our animals, our hearts shatter when the ones we love die. Grief possesses the ingredients and the power to break hearts. In this chapter we will consider the often messy nature of pet loss and the grief that entails. We'll look at how it is similar to—yet different from—the grief we feel when a loved human dies.

We, the ones left, our hands pressed tight against our chest, feel our hearts crack: we are the bereaved, the ones who grieve. The term *grief* has a number of meanings. It comes from the Latin word *gravis*, meaning "heavy" or "weighty." Old French *grever* means to "afflict, burden, oppress." Don't we feel like that—burdened, weighed down by heaviness, finding it difficult to get up each day and to go through the motions of daily, ordinary living? Nothing is "normal" anymore, and we struggle under a heaviness of body, emotions, and spirit.

The word *bereavement* comes from the Old English *bereafian*, which means to "seize," to "be deprived of," to "take away," or even to be "robbed." Bereft, we may feel that we have been "robbed" of our loved ones, certainly deprived of their presence, their barks or meows, their smell, their fur. The root word *reave* means "torn apart." Sometimes the death of a loved one causes physical pain. Losing a loved one can hurt because it feels as though you have been injured or have undergone an amputation. After the death of our beloved pet, we may feel as though one of our limbs has been ripped off.

After all, as we've discussed, we wrestle with whether to call them our pets, our animal companions, our fur family, our animal guardians, or our soul mates. Names can never encapsulate the breadth and depth of this interspecies love, of this gift that enables us to experience something of "the other" and to be blessed by "our familiar." Our animals are both other and familiar. We can know something of their lives with us, but there will always be deep mystery too. Death is mystery—the death of loved ones, the death of loved animal companions, and our own death.

This is yet another way that animals are teachers. Perhaps your pet has taught you patience or trust (and maybe that lesson is learning to trust again, which can be very difficult). Perhaps they've taught you to forgive, to embrace others, or to share the joy of walking in the wind, of slowing down so your dog may lift his leg, of stopping to smell the flowers, or of noting the seasons. In a sense, if we are prepared to follow the lead of our animals, we savor the simple pleasures of life, scaled down until only the essentials are within our vision: shelter, food, and, most importantly, *love*. Dare I suggest that as we grieve the loss of a loved animal companion, we also learn a little about death, and prepare or ready ourselves for when we embark on that mysterious journey too?

We grieve because we love.

It is as simple, and at the same time as complicated, as that. If we didn't love, we wouldn't grieve.

> *What I do know is that Brady will be a golden and*
> *enduring thread in the tapestry that is our memory. She*
> *was our first family dog, and we will never forget her.*
> —Client

A History of Grief

Grieving for a much-loved animal companion is nothing new. It is not due to our modern-day acceptance of pets or even of more recent times of lockdowns and restrictions during the COVID-19 pandemic, when we felt extra fortunate for animal-companion company and routines to keep us focused (yet their deaths during this time were often harder to bear, a topic I will address later). We humans have grieved the deaths of beloved animal companions for a long, long time. Ancient Egyptians shaved off their eyebrows after the death of their cats. This served as a visible sign of mourning and functioned as a calendar, specifying the period of mourning. They grieved until their eyebrows regrew! It was also a way to alert others to their grief. The lack of eyebrows may have served an additional function: to signal that physically the person has changed. This constitutes both physical (visible) and emotional (invisible) changes.

In Homer's epic poem, the *Odyssey*, we read a story that continues to resonate with dog lovers today. Alongside the more well-known stories about Odysseus—the sacking of Troy, the many adventures he experienced on his journey home from the Trojan War—is the story of the ancient bond between human animal and nonhuman animal. After a twenty-year absence, Odysseus returns home, disguised as a beggar. His old dog, Argos, lying in a pile of cow manure, neglected and flea-ridden, recognizes his master and wags his tail. Odysseus is unable to greet him because it would give away his identity. Instead, Odysseus, visibly moved, with tears in his eyes, walks past Argos. Argos then dies, having fulfilled his destiny, that of waiting for his master to return. Granted, this is a fine and moving story from the Greek classics, but I admit that I am frustrated by Odysseus! I want to remind him of his dog's loyalty and faithfulness, which I hope would change the story from Argos's death to Odysseus's hug. If the tale's outcome could not be altered, at least let the elderly, faithful Argos die in Odysseus's arms, surrounded by love.

Where was Argos's burial site? Did Odysseus mark the grave of his loyal friend? Argos may have been confined to the lines of an epic poem, perhaps symbolizing the preciousness of loyalty, but a number of ancient animal–human burial sites have been uncovered. Several of these sites have been found in the Middle East. In 2018, the 6,000-year-old bones of a domesticated dog were found in a tomb in northwestern Saudi Arabia, alongside what were probably the bones of its owners. Another ancient human–dog burial, with an older date of approximately twelve thousand years old, was discovered at Ain Mallaha, in Israel.

The oldest known burial plot of a domesticated dog was found not in the Middle East, however, but in Germany. This grave, dated at approximately fourteen thousand years old, was uncovered in 1914, in Oberkassel, which is now a suburb of Bonn. These old graves and likely formal burials speak of a deep bond between dog and human. But ancient graves can speak to the bond with the broader animal kingdom. In 2005, a burial plot of a man and a pet *fox* was found in Uyun-al-Hammam, in northern Jordan. The site is thought to be 16,500 years old. Researchers suggest that the man's pet fox was there to accompany his master to the afterlife. If this fox was indeed a pet, or an animal companion, then foxes may have been pets for several thousand years before dogs.

Of course, dogs (and foxes) were not the only animals buried, with or without a human. The oldest cat and human burial, thought to be approximately 9,500 years old, was found on the island of Cyprus. This is interesting for a number of reasons, one being that cats are not native to Cyprus. The cat would have been brought from the mainland. Therefore, it was more than likely domesticated, not wild.

Why have I started out writing about graves? How does this help? It reminds us that mourning for animal companions is nothing new. We know that animals became domesticated after showing humans their uses: dogs helped humans to hunt, guarded the camp, consumed offal and bits of the carcass humans didn't eat, and were sources of warmth. Cats also displayed their skills at keeping down the vermin population and thereby protected valuable grain stores from being eaten. In some countries cats also stopped mice from nibbling papyrus and paper and aided in hunting. Domestication worked for both sides. Companionship would have been another benefit. Whether it was named as such at the time, particularly in ancient times, is another matter.

Service and Therapy Animals: Community Ripples of Grief

Particular breeds of dogs that nowadays we might refer to as "lap dogs" often had other roles. Chihuahuas, for instance, functioned as guard dogs. They were carried on a person's back, in a type of blanket, their yap warning humans of approaching enemies. However, for the most part, our animal companions today do not have to work very hard. Of course, some do have jobs: as farm workers, search-and-rescue dogs, drug-detecting dogs, law-enforcement and military dogs, and assistance or therapy dogs.

In fact, these days, "assistance dogs" or "therapy dogs" are descriptive, yet broad, names used to categorize their work. This includes dogs who act as "eyes" for people with impaired vision, dogs who help those with hearing impairments, and dogs who assist humans with a wide spectrum of other disabilities. Some dogs go into hospitals and care facilities to visit patients and residents. Others go into schools to assist reluctant readers. My blind dog Harry is a "story dog." He goes into a school one day a week to listen to students read to him. It is a hard life: sprawled out on a rug on the school library couch, being read to, getting pats from students, plus treats.

The death of an assistance dog, then, has a ripple effect, grief moving out from the human family unit to include the person who has the disability, as well as the various organizations or charities, and their trainers and sponsors. For dogs whose work was centered more on visitation, the impact would be felt not only by the "owner" but by the community the dog used to visit, be it school, hospital, or nursing home.

If your animal companion was a service or therapy dog or involved in a program that assisted people in the community, then your working day and its routine have changed dramatically. You and your dog had a purpose, worked as a team. If your dog was taken into a school as a reading dog, or into a hospital, care facility, or hospice, then grief and loss extend into another community. Your assistance or therapy dog had relationships outside your home, with other people besides yourself and your immediate family. In the majority of these places, news of the death of your animal companion will need to be told to those in that community, who will also be affected by the loss of your companion animal. Some of these groups will have their own guidelines concerning how to handle this. Some will invite the human part of the team to come in to talk to the children or residents. Others will have one of the staff members break the news. Setting policies and procedures aside, the animal's death, and its impact on that particular group of people, needs to be acknowledged, not ignored or viewed as too painful to tell others. Even if the dog visited a dementia ward, one never knows what someone with dementia understands or does not understand, even if only in that moment. Children, too, feel the loss of a visiting dog. Even if they did not read to the story dog, they may have been at the school assembly when the dog was introduced to the school community, read about the dog in the school newsletter, or seen the dog being led between classrooms. Sometimes the death of a story dog is handled as part of a general school assembly. Sometimes the teacher or school counselor talks to the classes affected. Sometimes they're accompanied by the human part of the story-dog team. No matter how it's handled, this is an opportunity to speak about grief.

For the owner of a service dog, a sense of purpose has now gone. The rhythm for the week has changed. For the human, being cut off from their voluntary work can mean a decrease in their social and community outlet. This may lead to isolation, a feeling of being cut off from that group, and the loss of not interacting with the community members in the same way again.

Some will acquire another dog that will be trained to be an assistance dog, but this takes time. Some organizations will not allow a new dog to be tested for suitability until the dog has been in the household for at least a year. For others, it may not be possible to adopt or bring another dog into the household, or the new addition may not be deemed suitable to be a reading or therapy dog. This can be an added grief.

For those whose dogs were their own assisted-therapy dogs, there will be a huge loss, with its own accompanying grief. As therapy dogs age, this would have been anticipated, often with the dog being "retired" and a newly trained one entering the household. But this doesn't make the loss of a beloved therapy dog any easier. Most therapy-dog assistance groups have a social worker or counselor on staff to help the grieving owner navigate their way through grief and to help them in the training of their new service dog.

I know that a new dog is sometimes referred to as the "replacement," but I have problems with the use of that word. No animal—or human—can ever replace a former one. They may look the same in terms of color and breed, but they are not the same. We have heard of parents going out to "replace" a guinea pig or rabbit or fish when they died. But the child usually knows! (See chapter 3 for more on this.) How can one "replace" a personality? A bond? It is also part of the dilemma when we may hear, "It was only a dog [or cat or fish]. You can get another one." Correct me if I am wrong, but following the death of a spouse, no one would say, "It was only a husband, you can go and get another one."

Types of Grief

Our dogs (and other animals) love us, for the most part, unconditionally —they don't carry baggage about us. When a human dies, unresolved issues or complicated relationships may compound our grief. Unlike many human relationships, in the majority of cases, our animal companions just love us the way we already are—not how they want us to be (mind you, my cat would like me to open the refrigerator a little more frequently and go to bed earlier!). It really is pure grief, grief that is not offset by our foibles, flaws, or failings.

One type of grief, which can be quite disabling, is known as disenfranchised grief. This is grief that is not acknowledged or is overlooked by society. This lack of support or acknowledgment can leave people frustrated, again, wondering if they are "normal," and can lead to isolation. Unfortunately, there are individuals in our local communities—perhaps friends, neighbors, or work colleagues—who don't understand why you are grieving.

No one can know how you are feeling, the depths of your grief, the things you are missing. There is a risk that you may close yourself off to others, preventing or ending these hurtful comments. Instead of running the risk of becoming bitter, or resentful, or damaging an otherwise lovely friendship, I suggest that you think of the joys of having a pet as being on the same plane as learning a foreign language—or being visited by an alien. In other words, just as we can't understand languages we don't speak or visits from creatures unproven to exist, non-animal-loving people can't understand the grief. So cut them some slack.

What I find helpful, and less abrasive, is feeling sorry for them, for they have missed out on one of life's biggest joys—bonding with an animal companion and sharing your life with them.

You may even say, or feel, that your heart has broken. A broken heart. You are not imagining it. It is a real condition. There is even a medical name for it: Takotsubo cardiomyopathy, or "broken-heart syndrome." The left ventricle of the heart is weakened, or temporarily stunned, usually as the result of severe stress. This is why you may feel a dull ache or pain or even notice a shortness of breath. Grief hurts. You may indeed experience physical pain. It is not something you have imagined. If it continues or worsens, you may need to seek medical help, to speak to your doctor.

One of the reasons we grieve so deeply for our animal companions is because they were in our environment 24/7. If you went out to work, they were there to greet you at the door on your return. During the COVID-19 pandemic, they sat by your desk while you worked and on the couch, by your side, when you relaxed. So much of your home has associations with your animal friend. The scuff marks on the floorboards, the little dip on the sofa, the place where their bed was, the place for the water bowl. I will look at these factors in more depth later, but at this stage I would like you to acknowledge that the grief you are experiencing (or fearing—if you are reading this book in preparation) is normal and real and a sign of your bond and of your love.

Grief is an emotion; it cannot be turned off because someone thinks you have had long enough to "get over" the death of your pet. Western society does not deal with grief very well. I notice the advertisements on the television. The anti-aging creams and lotions are a subconscious pull, products that suggest that, if we remain youthful in appearance, then death remains at bay (this assumes that death only visits the elderly). Even some advertisements for life insurance are deceptive. One in Australia talks about the benefits of having life insurance, the voiceover saying, "*If* you die . . ." not "*When* you die . . ."

Theologian Joan Chittister writes that "grief is a sign that we loved something more than ourselves." Or, as Winnie the Pooh put it: "How lucky I am to have something that makes saying goodbye so hard."

How true that is! Have we said, or thought, that we would trade places with our pet if it would save their life? I have, and you probably have said or thought that too. We love them deeply, and it feels as if we love them more than we love ourselves. We are not alone in thinking those thoughts. Reflect back on the stories you may have read or seen on television of people going into burning houses or otherwise risking their lives to try to save their pets.

Before we look more closely at grief, and what aspects may be present, it is important to stress that grief is *not* a disease that needs to be cured or a problem that is to be solved. Grief is a process that is the flipside of love, and it is a condition that is to be *supported*. Grief is a normal response to loss, to the absence of a loved one. It is also important to underline that there is no timeline or time frame. One does not "get over" grief. We adjust to life, but grief accompanies us. We never "get over it" or "complete" a particular time frame (such as a month or a year).

Several key factors play a part in determining how we grieve. Grief, and the way each of us grieves, is influenced by our personality, the circumstances of the death, the depth or importance of the bond, our previous experiences of grief, and what level of support is on offer. Having said that, no grief is the same, because no dog, cat, bird, fish, or person is the same and no life experience is the same. The way we grieve for pets in our lives can be quite different because each experience, each relationship, is unique.

Think about growing up. I know parents are not meant to have favorites, but your mother or father may have bonded more deeply with one of your siblings than with you. This didn't mean (I hope) that your sister or brother was loved more than you; it might have been because your parent had more in common with your sibling or was of a similar personality. It is vital to keep this at the forefront of your mind as we consider diverse and multifaceted ways we may grieve for our animal companions: differences do not mean an absence or lessening of love.

> *I still put my hand out in the night thinking I will feel his soft fur or gentle little paws. He was such a gentle cat. For a long time, he was my best friend. I could tell him anything and he understood. I am so lonely without my little darling.*
>
> —Client

Personality and Emotions

Grief is affected by your personality, and the personality of your much-loved animal companion. How would you describe yourself? Your pet? Are you outgoing or more of an introvert? What about your animal companion? Were they always on the go, wanting to be part of the action, or would they prefer to keep close to you, perhaps curled up at your feet, or following you, assuming the title of your "little shadow"?

If we are more outgoing, we may find it easier to express our emotions, but not always. Feelings are part of the grief cocktail and important to acknowledge. You may not be comfortable owning some of these feelings, such as anger. You may be scared by anger or believe you should not be experiencing it, or if you feel it, it should have a tight lid on it. Well, welcome to the grief party, where many emotions just show up uninvited!

Sometimes families find it difficult to mourn openly, or as a collective unit, because family members grieve differently. It is important to remember this when the time comes to grieve the loss of a family pet. Some members may shut down, pushing their emotions deep down, perhaps even appearing not to care. They may not wish to participate in a ceremony or look through photographs together. Others are more open, and there's no need to guess how they are feeling—they are showing it! Those who are more outgoing or gregarious may cope or adjust sooner than the quieter ones. They may be more willing to seek help, or talk about their feelings with another.

In the 1970s, Elisabeth Kübler-Ross set out what has become known as "the five stages of grief." According to Kübler-Ross (and earlier researchers), emotions associated with grief could include denial, anger, bargaining, depression, and acceptance. Later, this five-stage model was expanded to seven, with the inclusion of shock (as the first on the list) and testing (between depression and acceptance). While the five stages of grief followed a type of movement, once the other two stages were added, this was no longer the case. The additions highlighted the fact that grief is not linear or stable; there is no right or wrong way to grieve, no right or wrong way to feel. Contrary to the way the Kübler-Ross approach has been interpreted, we don't always start out in shock, then go through denial, proceeding through the individual stages until we have arrived at acceptance of grief. Although Kübler-Ross did not set out her model of the stages of grief to be linear, many have mistakenly interpreted them this way. People are not expected to experience all the stages while grieving, or even in a particular order. Indeed, the feelings, or stages, may differ depending on the type, or depth, of bereavement. These "stages" were meant to be descriptive, not prescriptive.

While this model can be helpful, it's a fairly clinical way to describe what is a matter of the heart. During loss we experience a rollercoaster of different emotions, sometimes seeming to come out of nowhere! Stages are not confined to a set period of time; they can erupt at different times and places. You may be angry that your cat died, and years later that anger may resurface because you have just bought a new house that your cat would have loved.

How the stages manifest also differs from person to person. The stage of bargaining can be loaded, and seemingly only appropriate if one believes in a higher power: "If you save my dog, God, I will do whatever you want me to . . ." The added stage of testing is about considering different ways to manage grief—how to crawl out of the black hole of depression. Not everyone will suffer depression. Depression is quite different from sadness and may need medical intervention. Sadness may not need help from a medical practitioner, because sadness usually lifts over time, with support from family and friends and with self-care measures put in place. (If it doesn't lessen, please visit your doctor.) Not everyone will experience shock. You may have been preparing for weeks, or even months, because your animal companion was old or ill. Our emotions will sometimes show themselves suddenly and quite unexpectedly. When one is grieving, the seven (or five) stages of grief can be helpful in terms of recognizing some of the emotions you may feel, but you do not necessarily proceed through them in a linear fashion, or necessarily feel all of them.

The Faces and Stages of Grief

Let us consider some feelings, and their accompanying actions, that are associated with grief.

> *Not traveling too well. . . . Sometimes I just cry on trains or while I'm walking down the street. I can't seem to stop looking for Lucy and wanting her back and missing her.*
>
> —Client

Sometimes we hear, and take on board, the message that unless someone is crying, then they are not grieving. This is unfounded and wrong. Some people cry openly and are unable to control their tears. Others are quiet, bottling it up. Think of a sad movie, or a movie that produces happy tears. Not everyone in the theater is in tears, are they? The same is the case when a loved one (human or nonhuman) dies. I have stood next to people who did not shed a tear when and after their animal companion was euthanized. This doesn't mean they didn't care. Some are not criers. Others may be more private and prefer to shed tears in the car or when they arrive home. I have met many who were worried that if they cried, they would be unable to stop. No tears does not equal no grief. This is important, because it can help you when you are called on to support someone. It is time to rid ourselves of these stereotypes concerning grief.

What about other stereotypes? Do we think the more burly or muscular the male, the less likely the tears? I have seen tall, bulky, tattooed, school-of-hard-knocks-type men break down and sob when their pets have died.

What I will say about tears is that crying is *one* physical display of grief. I have heard clients say that they are "all cried out" or "I couldn't possibly have any more tears left in me." Depending on the nature of their pet's death, it could have been a long illness, and the tears have been shed during those weeks or months; the crying has already happened—but not the grieving.

Sadness is an emotion that may be accompanied by outer tears or by inner crying. This can be an intense time. Thoughts such as *How can I live without my loyal friend?* partnered with a sense of what it means to be absent from your loved one, can make day-to-day life painful. If one is working or can keep occupied during the day (the mantra "I have to keep busy" is a common one), the lid on sadness can be shut for a time, but come evening, the emotions resurface, ready to spring out like a caged tiger finally set free.

Sadness can be accompanied by loneliness, because grieving may cause one to self-isolate. It may become too hard to keep explaining to others how you are feeling, and again, being worried you might open the floodgates and never stop crying. You don't want to make others uncomfortable, so you keep to yourself.

Anger is another intense emotion, one that may make you feel uncomfortable or even prompt you to deny its existence, to protest that "I am *not* angry!" Anger can be the manifestation of frustration, frustration that nothing could be done by the veterinarian to prolong or save the life of your loved pet. Sometimes it can be hard to identify the source of the anger; it can be as simple as the shortness of nonhuman life spans, which means we will end up living much of our lives without them, or it can be as complicated as feeling we've failed our pets.

I remember a client who was distraught, her feelings of anger compounded by the knowledge of the care she had received from her dog during her own battle with breast cancer. Sobbing, she told me that her dog had got her through her treatment, lying next to her on her bed for weeks during her time of recovery. Now her dog had been diagnosed with an inoperable, aggressive tumor. She had come to the heart-wrenching decision to euthanize her pet. She could remember how ill she had been during chemotherapy and how long it took to recover from surgery. She didn't want to put her much-loved, loyal animal companion through that.

Often anger is partnered with guilt. This client's anger at what she perceived as a great injustice was probably accompanied by a large dollop of guilt, in this instance, due to the nature of her animal companion's illness. Anger and guilt: a happy pair! We humans are prone to rummaging through our actions or replaying them over and over again, thinking we have made a mistake. The guilt may be because of a time issue: "If only I'd taken my dog in earlier . . ." "If only I'd been there instead of at work . . ." "I should have known . . ."

We beat ourselves up. The regrets make us sound as though we are all-knowing, omniscient. I don't know about you, but when I look into a mirror, I see a flawed, human being, not God. If our animals could talk to us, if they could tell us exactly where they hurt, if they could tell us if the medication helped them with pain or if it made them feel sick, *if . . . if . . . if . . .* The answers to all those words would make their lives and our lives easier, but this does not happen. So we, as their guardians, as their best friends, have to make decisions, usually accompanied by veterinary advice, to help relieve their suffering. Yes, sometimes we have left off making decisions, but that is usually because our heart does not want to hear what our head is trying to tell us.

In those instances, be gentle with yourself. I strongly believe that in the majority of cases, the decisions we make concerning our animal companions are the correct ones at the time. If your personality is one that tends to look back or if your mantra becomes "If only . . ." or "I should have . . .," then this guilt may be particularly hard to let go of. Try to stop looking back. We are meant to focus on what is ahead, in front. I like to think of a monster made up of rear-view mirrors. If this sounds like *your* monster, picture yourself covering it with a dark cloth. Stop the reproaches and believe that you did the best you could at the time with the information you had.

Having said that, occasionally the decision to euthanize can come down to financial constraints, particularly if the pet is going to need costly or complicated surgery (perhaps with a poor prognosis), chemotherapy, or ongoing medical treatment. It is not for us to judge. Healthcare is costly for humans as well as for animals. It would be a wonderful world indeed if money didn't have to be part of decision-making concerning healthcare. If you have to euthanize for these reasons and there is no other option, then remember it is not a perfect world; making that decision doesn't mean you don't love your pet.

If guilt arises because of an accident (sadly, many of our animal companions do get hit by vehicles or are injured or die because of dog attacks), acknowledge it, saying, "I am sorry," in your heart. If there is a lesson to be learned (such as the lock needs fixing on the gate, to always have your dog on a lead when outside your property, or being cautious around unfamiliar dogs), tuck that information away. Try to feel a sense of forgiveness, dependent upon your spiritual or religious tradition.

One of the stages of grief that was added to the initial five was shock. We use that word a lot, don't we? "I was shocked by . . ." "Such a shock!" In terms of grief, feeling shock protects us. Our bodies shut down, our minds close off, and we become physically, emotionally, and perhaps also spiritually "numb." Numbing is a bit like an overcoat for intense feelings. Shock prevents, or shelters, us from feelings of intense pain until we are a little more ready for it, perhaps even allowing us to arrive home after being at the vet, to be at home or with family. We may hear others say, "I didn't feel anything," or you may have experienced that yourself. Sometimes a client of mine would question their love for the deceased because they felt nothing at the time. If I spoke to them several days later, it was usually a very different story. Think about when you cut yourself with a vegetable knife. You may not feel pain for several seconds, but then it kicks in. The shock of grief can be like that.

Shock signals a battle taking place between the head and the heart: in your head you know that your animal companion has died, but in your heart you don't believe it yet. The battle is between intellectual acceptance of reality and the emotional struggle. Events may be blurry, or you may feel it is almost an "out-of-body" experience. It is happening, but you are experiencing it as an observer, not as a participant. There is disconnection, detachment. This is why it is important to put off making significant decisions, at least for several days. The decision you may need to make might be how to care for the bodily remains of your loved one. You may need time to think, to work out the best option for you. If you haven't thought about this, you may need several days of thinking and reflecting, days when you are not so shocked and numb. I would advise taking this time to make up your mind, even if you have already decided, so you can approach it with a fresh mind and a firmness of decision. Most vets, cremation services, and pet cemeteries understand this and would also suggest that you take several days to make up your mind, to make sure that what you think now is what your decision will be in three days' time. Shock not only prevents the making of important decisions (or any decision, really); it also highlights your vulnerability to undertake simple tasks. There is a reduced level of functioning.

When intense feelings surface, these can lead to exhaustion, worsening of preexisting medical conditions, and, in some cases, suicidal thoughts, especially if depression is present. There may also be a range of physical symptoms. Some people experience shortness of breath. High anxiety may be accompanied by tightness in the chest, hypertension, and a faint or thready pulse. One may experience an urge to be sick, or may be cold and clammy (common symptoms with shock). Other physical symptoms could be a tightness in the throat, an oversensitivity to noise and light, muscle weakness, a dry mouth, and a lack of energy. Headaches, stomachaches, constipation (or the opposite, diarrhea), blurred vision, weight loss or weight gain, an urgency to urinate more often, and fatigue are all common byproducts of grief—as are, of course, sleep disturbances.

Complicated or Unresolved Grief

It never hurts to underline what I said earlier: grief is a normal reaction to loss. Having said that, there are terms associated with grief that may imply it is a condition or syndrome. You may have heard or read literature that speaks of grief being "complicated" or "unresolved." I have a few problems with the use of these terms.

Of course grief is complicated. It involves intense feelings, which may be accompanied by a number of physical symptoms or manifestations. Grief, by its very nature, is complicated. When we love and that love has died (or gone away), then we are left navigating our way through an unexplored maze. Yes, you may have grieved before—for a parent, a partner, or another animal companion—but every grief is different because every loved one is different—be they human or nonhuman. Your previous experiences may help or hinder you, as you anticipate and make your way through new territory, but it is still different.

Grief, by its very essence and nature, is also "unresolved." One does not "resolve" grief. I prefer to think that we learn to cope with our daily living, in the presence of grief. Grief does not go away, it isn't a disease that can be cured, and grieving for a long period of time does not mean there is something the matter with you. The terms *unresolved grief* and *complicated grief* imply that there are opposites— uncomplicated grief and resolved grief. *All* grief is unresolved (the loved one is no longer with us physically) and living through grief is complicated, messy, hard. Eventually one learns to live with grief, but one does not "get over" grief and there is no set time frame for the progress, healing, or resolution of grief.

Another loaded term is *closure*. Closure implies that there will be a time when the grief has finished. Closure suggests a limit for grief. I prefer to use the word *acceptance*. We may eventually accept that we are suffering loss, accepting that we will always miss our loved one(s). Closure implies there will be a time when the grief has ended or finished. We will always miss our loved ones, whether they had legs, fur, or fins.

There can, however, be *anticipatory grief*, when we know that the life of our dear animal friend is drawing to a close. This may be due to a medical condition, age, or not recovering from an accident. We anticipate that there will be death and, in a sense, prepare for the loss. But we can never ready ourselves adequately or sufficiently to

accept the upcoming physical separation. We should not underestimate the emotional heaviness that may accompany anticipatory grief.
This feeling, anxiety even, may have started to accompany you once
your loved one became ill. We start preparing in our minds, and in
our homes, offering special diets, medication, perhaps discouraging
jumping up on a couch due to a bad back, hip problems, or arthritis.
Maybe your animal companion is becoming visually impaired or deaf,
so furniture is not moved and markers, textured fabric, or scents may
be used to help them find their way around their home.

Grieving a Pet versus Grieving a Human

There are a number of differences in the way we might grieve the
death of a pet versus the death of a human. The first concerns that
of an emotion, which I have already addressed, but wish to explore
further. Here the emotion of guilt is considered in terms of making
the decision to euthanize or put an animal companion "to sleep" when
it is suffering, ill, or dying. I have had many clients cry, "I killed my
best friend," or "I know I did the right thing, but why does it feel so
wrong?"

Guilt is an underlying emotion in much of pet loss. If we reached
the difficult decision to euthanize our pet, we may ask, "Did we do the
right thing?" Or we question if they were really ready to go, or if we
should have waited another day, week, or month. We wish our pets could
have told us they were ready—in words, rather than looks. Sometimes
family is brought into the guilt-play as well, saying things like, "You were
never as close to her as I was. You don't understand," or "If you had been
here, I wouldn't have had to take him to the vet on my own."

Perhaps you did not find out about the life-threatening disease
until it was too late to cure. Diseases in animals, including timelines

and rates of progression, can differ from those in humans. Speak to your veterinarian for more information, especially if you are feeling guilty that you "missed" some clue about an underlying illnesss or condition. Perhaps you wondered whether you let it go too long before seeking vet help, euthanasia, or other interventions. As I have already mentioned, euthanasia may have come about due to finances; veterinary costs are not cheap, and not everyone can afford veterinary care or all forms of veterinary care. However, sometimes euthanasia happens because of a move. Maybe you think adjusting to a move will be too much for your elderly dog, or you are having to euthanize because you are moving into aged care and there is no one to care for your pet. Sometimes the pet has had to be euthanized because he or she has bitten someone or has become aggressive. Euthanasia means "good death," but that isn't always the case, is it? Sometimes the circumstances that lead to euthanasia seem less than good and come with the heavy baggage of guilt.

Perhaps the guilt is because you were unable to be present during the euthanasia. Not everyone can be, for all sorts of reasons. Some clients decline to be present because they are afraid that their tears and sobbing will distress their pet. Others want to remember their pet as they were when alive. Other reasons can be as simple (but as real and significant) as being afraid of needles or fainting at a medical procedure. Other clients prefer to stay outside with family members, perhaps sharing words and hugs, or saying a short prayer during the time the euthanasia is being performed.

As I mentioned earlier, guilt may come about because of the pet's illness, or cause of death. Sadly, another way that pet death differs (for the most part) from human death is when a pet goes missing or is found dead. This also happens for humans, but it is not as common (I in no way intend to downplay this tragedy). Untimely death, or the disappearance of a pet, can be disturbing, particularly under tragic circumstances, such as being killed in a car accident, killed by another animal, killed due to violence, or being stolen or going missing. These situations can give rise to overwhelming crashing waves, tidal in impact, of deep guilt. Questions such as "What could I have done to prevent this loss?" or "Why wasn't I watching where he was walking?" arise, as does the blame game by thinking, *If I had been home, this wouldn't have happened.*

If your animal companion has gone missing, not knowing what has happened can be horrible. Most of the time we imagine the worst scenarios and are relieved when our lost ones are found. Many years ago our cat went exploring next door and managed to get herself locked in our neighbor's van. A very relieved cat was returned to us at the end of the day. Another time our gate was open due to workmen. It was a harrowing five days, but eventually we were contacted, our "missing" signs around the neighbourhood bearing much-wanted fruit! (Note: If your cat has run off, be aware that most cats will not come when called if outside their home. Try setting out their food or a litter box instead.)

It is a good security measure to make sure your pets have current tags and are microchipped. Sometimes it is easy to forget to update them if you have moved or have a different mobile number. It's best practice to add "update microchip/tags details" to your moving "to do" list. If your pet does go missing, contact local veterinarians and animal shelters. Use social media, plus old-fashioned posters in your local area.

Unfortunately, as is the case when a missing human is never found, questions such as "What if . . .?" can plague us. If you are finding it difficult to cope, please seek professional help.

Occasionally, a pet may die while receiving medical treatment in an animal hospital. This can be particularly distressing for owners, especially if the pet appeared to be recovering or doing well. Of course, the same can happen with human patients, but a major difference is that there are usually more restricted visiting hours in animal hospitals. Many do not allow an owner to sit by an animal's cage for hours on end (a marked contrast to the practice in many hospitals, which allow the next of kin/close family members to sit by the bed of a very ill, or dying patient, for as long as they like).

> *For the first couple of weeks I would say, "Oh I better*
> *go feed the dogs," expecting Cloud to come to the back*
> *door, with her nose pressed against the door.*
>
> —Client

Grief Triggers at Home

When one returns home, the daily routine adds its own grief. Many of us say that our animal companions are our best cheerleaders; they love us unconditionally. If you really want to see the difference between animal and human, leave the room where your pet and your human partner or family are. Enter the room in about five minutes' time. Who came to greet you? Who missed you? Who didn't know you had even left the room? (The human is the answer for this last one!)

Now, I know there are human family members who try (and we love that they try!), but they are unable to love us with that devotion, undivided loyalty, undying love, which also forgives us our faults and flaws. Our animal companions never ruminate and wonder why we can't be more like them. When they die, we miss that boost to our self-confidence, that assurance that we are loved for who we are, not for our bank balance, our address, our looks, our clothing sense, our education, our job. Ever seen a person living on the street with their dog? That dog loves them for their core, for their very being. The dog doesn't judge them or sum them up by society's standards.

Home. It's hard. Your home was your pet's home too. There are physical reminders everywhere: beds, feeding bowls, fur, maybe a nail or two near the scratching post, nose marks on windows, photographs.

As one of my clients said, "We miss our dog's gentle little presence around the house. I still can't get used to the fact that she won't be there when I come home, wagging her tail and greeting me as she did for nearly sixteen years."

Another client said, "We feel our cat's spirit and soul will always remain with us. She is in every room in the house and all her favorite spots in the garden, but still, it hurts. She will remain in our hearts always."

These sentiments make sense. Our homes were their homes, and there are reminders everywhere. Your animal companion probably set up your daily routine: feed, walk, brush, etc. These daily tasks at times helped you, or another human, through tough times. After I had recovered sufficiently from major surgery, I remember being so happy when I could at last walk my dog. Life was getting back to normal. Some clients confided that their pets, needing to be fed and looked after, helped them get out of bed in the morning, helped ease their mental health issues.

Having been their caregiver, you might find unexpected prompts triggering your grief and tears. Going to the supermarket can open up the tear ducts. Even if you avoid the pet food aisle, even if you didn't buy your food from this particular supermarket, you do run the risk of seeing pet food and pictures of pets. You may have successfully steered clear of the pet food aisle, but coming around the corner of another aisle, you notice a display of pet food on special. Even arriving at the checkout, realizing that your weekly grocery load is smaller, that pet-food tins were not being unloaded to be scanned, can be a stark reminder of what is missing, what has changed, what you have lost.

Going for a walk, even just leaving your place of residence to get into your car, can also be a trigger. You may realize you would have taken your dog with you for the drive. Or you see other dogs out for a walk. It isn't that you want *that* dog; you're not jealous. You want your own one, your deceased loved one, and you miss that physical routine that kept you both fit and active.

Your animal companion may have added layers of human connections. Your pet may have been your deceased partner's pet or a wedding or anniversary gift. Sometimes the pet is a reminder of happier times, before a divorce or a breakup, and you may have had to battle to win custody. Sometimes the link is to another tragedy, to another death, or to a child who no longer lives at home.

Let us not forget that, for many, animal companions are not only family, but they are referred to in language which denotes a relationship akin to that of a parent/child. Consider some of the things my clients have told me:

> *Not many people understand how some people can love their pets the way myself and my family do, each one of them was so important to each of us and the void each has left can never be filled. . . . I can only hope and pray that you are right and that our three precious pets that brought so much love and warmth into my family are now together, suffering no more.*

> *Our hearts still ache every time we think of our beloved dog Sam. We feel that he's around us. It's hard to believe that he has gone forever . . . I hope we can meet each other in the*

*other side of the rainbow like we want to see all the members
in the family, because Sam's just like our other son.*

*It really means a lot to me that people actually care and think
of their pets as part of their family as we have been for our
beloved Jerry. I'm still missing him from my life and think of
him every day. He was my little boy!*

*My life is empty without my little boy, but I know he is free
from pain and suffering.*

Poignantly, this may be the relationship owned and acknowledged by those without human children. One client told me, "We now have our lovely Harry resting peacefully in our garden at home and each time we pass him on our day-to-day activities we think of him and the wonderful sixteen years of memories we have of our beautiful man. As we don't have children the loss of Harry is felt deeper, and it's only people who either own pets or work with them who know the sense of loss and sadness."

Another client said, "I don't have children of my own, so my animals are my children. I had Bessie from the day she was born as I had her father and mother, so Bessie was extra special to me."

As I mentioned earlier, pet loss involves the whole family, but often in myriad ways. We may grieve differently, but also the activities we were involved in with our animal companion may have been quite distinct. Unless we consciously reflect on this, perhaps writing down the various modes of interaction for each family member, we may not recognize what might become potential grief trigger points.

Consider what one client wrote to me after I sent them a card with the "Rainbow Bridge" poem:

Your lovely thoughts and words on the day we lost our Jenny
were received by us just at the right time as the kids and I
really were not dealing well with Jenny no longer being here
with us. She was a part of all of us and we are still grieving
for her. I know we did the right thing as do all of us here, but
I just cannot explain the hurt we are all feeling. Jimmy finds
it hard to go out into the backyard with Jenny no longer there
right behind him. Jason misses his ball game and playing with
her. Lucy still can't talk about her when she comes over. She
just wants to be able to cuddle and snuggle with her. Myself, I
really miss her love, I have a medical condition myself and am
often not well, Jenny always knew when I was having a bad
day and would cuddle into me and lick away my tears.

This letter illustrates the point very well. Playmate, companion, the "little shadow," the confidante, the comforter: what role or roles did your beloved pet have in your household? Even if you live on your own, you may have family members or friends who would name your animal as their friend, the one they took care of (and hung out with) when you went on vacation. If you do not have children, sometimes your parents may have referred to the dog or cat as their "fur grandchild." Sometimes animal companions act as the glue in a family, or as a neutral zone or diffusing point.

Sometimes animal companions bind us to those who have died. Recent death has a painful habit of digging up past griefs or sadness, exposing our hearts to the hurt again, opening the "starting to mend" flesh of our hearts. One client struggled with the loss of their cat, Tiger, as it opened up the wounds of losing their son.

Another factor that may come into play is previous experiences of grief. How did you handle them? What was helpful or unhelpful? Don't compare how you grieved then (or your memory of grieving; these can be two quite different things) with how you are grieving now. Grief doesn't happen in isolation. Life doesn't stop to allow us to grieve for someone, giving us an appropriate time frame before hitting us with another death. You may be experiencing multiple griefs: death, aging, loss of a job, health problems. As I have already said, you may have been grieving other losses that happened to your animal companion: blindness, deafness, aging, diabetes. Sometimes a recent grief rips off a bandage that has been covering up other losses in your life, which is why the deaths of other loved ones may feel particularly close to you during this time.

Another matter is that of support, which I will touch on in more detail in chapter 5. Don't hesitate to seek support; it is not a sign of weakness. If you do not have family nearby, or if your family does not understand (or grieve the way you do), is there a group or a close friend who will listen to you? Are family and friends understanding?

Remember to be kind to yourself, and to extend that kindness to others. No grief is identical, even if the death occurs within the same family. No one is the same, either human or nonhuman, and no one has the equivalent life experience as someone else. It is worth holding in your heart the words of a powerful First Nations saying: "Never judge another until you have walked a full moon in his/her moccasins." Yet, even so, we must recognize that we will never ever know someone else completely.

Be kind. Acknowledge your grief. As your hands clutch your chest, trying to hold together the sharp shards of your shattered heart, know that its breakage was brought about by powerful ammunition. Your aching heart was targeted by the strongest and most enduring emotion that there is: love.

As we've discussed, that love goes both ways. This story illustrates that love beautifully:

A dog spirit waiting to go to earth was trying out his
   moves for God. He raised an ear and let his tongue
   hang out.

"Humans love that," God replied.

"What about this?" the dog asked, chasing his tail.

"That makes them laugh," God replied.

"And this?" The dog fetched a ball.

"That makes them happy, too," God replied.

"Do I do anything that makes them sad?" the dog asked.

God thought about it, but couldn't speak for the lump in
   his throat.

"What?" the dog asked.

"Never mind," God replied. "I'll tell you when you get
   back."

HEARTBEAT

"My best friend, my dog Jennie, has died."

—Maurice Sendak

THE AMERICAN WRITER Maurice Sendak acquired a beautiful Sealyham terrier in 1953. This dog, named Mona Lisa by her breeders and renamed Jennie by Sendak, became one of Sendak's greatest loves. Some have pondered whether Sendak wanted a small breed of dog because he was short. Perhaps, but Sendak had other, much bigger dogs during his life, including a golden retriever and a number of German shepherds.

Jennie featured in a number of Sendak's books, including his most famous one, *Where the Wild Things Are.* In one illustration, Jennie is the model for the dog being chased down the stairs by Max, who is wielding a fork. Jennie also makes an appearance in other works by Sendak, including *Hector Protector*, in which she is portrayed as Queen Victoria's dog (and has her own crown).

These are all minor roles really, preparation for Jennie's own starring role, for she is the major character in *Higglety Pigglety Pop! or There Must Be More to Life*. This book is about Jennie, Sendak's tribute to her. Several of the illustrations, beautifully crosshatched, were based on photographs of Jennie: the frontispiece with Jennie sitting at the table, and another where she is looking out the window. The book was written when Jennie was old. She was soon to become very ill with cancer. Sendak was fearing her death. We could almost say that this book was written about anticipatory grief. Sendak said: "It was all a nightmare, but Jennie never complained. She wasn't a complaining dog." It was published a month after Jennie's death, and it is said that Sendak wept when he received his author's copies of the book.

From the beginning, there is no mistaking that this is a book about Jennie, and for Jennie. The first illustration has Jennie sitting at the table, surrounded by her medications. Nearby there is a food bowl with "Jennie" written on it. On the wall behind Jennie is a print of the *Mona Lisa*. If we are still in doubt, two pages in is the dedication: "For Jennie."

The title is taken from a nursery rhyme written by Samuel Griswold Goodrich, in 1846. Sendak's tale is melancholy, dealing with Jennie's angst. Jennie is dissatisfied with her life. She has everything, but knows she is missing something. She is wise, feeling that there is more to life than having everything. After several adventures, Jennie ends up in a theater troupe, known as The World Mother Goose Theatre, starring in the nursery rhyme: *Higglety Pigglety Pop!* Jennie plays the role of the dog. "The dog has eaten the mop," an actor says as the theater group performs in the park of a place known as the Castle Yonder.

Where, or indeed, what, is Castle Yonder? Written when Jennie was elderly, when Sendak's mother was dying from cancer, and after Sendak had suffered a cardiac arrest while overseas in England: well, Castle Yonder could be a reference to death or to the afterlife. In the epilogue, there is a hint: "Now Jennie has everything." No need for medication, she is performing every night, loving what she is doing. Jennie's life has been made complete through the journey through death.

The conclusion of the epilogue is in the form of a letter. The last two sentences contain a strong reference to heaven, and to the hope of seeing her master again. Jennie writes: "I can't tell you how to get to the

Castle Yonder because I don't know where it is. But if you ever come this way, look for me." In an earlier version, Sendak added, "Someday I will go see her."

Why did Sendak delete it? Would it have been too upsetting if readers understood the reference to death and assumed that Sendak was writing about his own death? He may have thought it too disturbing, so it was removed.

Sendak wrote a libretto for an opera based on the book in 1984, the musical score composed by Oliver Knussen. Sendak was also one of the set designers. In the opera, the stage design for Castle Yonder is of a ruin, a wonderful place for ghosts and spirits to dwell. It certainly seems to be a metaphor for death. Tony Kushner believes that the book (and libretto) is about "the dark country on the other side of death."

This book addresses grief (which is the flip side of deep love) and the painful absence of a loved one. Sendak's relationship with Jennie was extremely close. "Jennie was the love of my life," he said. Amid the pain, the story is hopeful, for we want to find the Castle Yonder, and meet up once more with all of our loved ones, regardless of species. Not every animal companion is fortunate enough to have a book penned about them, but their stories are written in and on the hearts of their owners.

Many of us can identify with Sendak, who, more than a year after Jennie's death, wrote: "I still dream of Jennie, and the pain is unrelenting."

2

SPIRITUAL HEARTS

Pets and the Afterlife

FOR MANY OF US, the death of a loved one unearths deep questions concerning immortality and the presence or hope of the existence of an afterlife. This can be even more pronounced when a loved animal companion has died. Unfortunately, we hear comments and read reports from people, religious and nonreligious, who state that animals have no souls and therefore do not participate in any form of afterlife; this means that there will be no reunion with their human companions.

It seems appropriate to pause to consider views from a number of religious and spiritual traditions. It is important to state the obvious: no one knows for certain the conditions of the afterlife; these remain matters of faith, belief, and mystery. Still, some of the greatest minds from history have weighed in on the debate. Greek mathematician and philosopher Pythagoras said, "Animals share with us the privilege of having a soul." Reformer Martin Luther wrote, "Be thou comforted, little dog, thou too in Resurrection shall have a little golden tail." And Robert Louis Stevenson wrote, "You think dogs will not be in heaven? I tell you, they will be there long before any of us."

When I began my role as chaplain in an animal hospital, some members of the church were dismissive, thinking that the majority of my ministry would entail patting pets on the head! A continuous "meet and greet." This was incorrect, and so far from what chaplaincy at an animal hospital actually entailed (the CEO was insistent that it was not "pet chaplaincy" because much of the time I provided ministry to humans, the pet owners). One of the most surprising yet deeply moving theological and spiritual components I encountered there were theological questions raised by clients, mostly from the "unchurched," but also from adherents of faith traditions. Their questions addressed core matters of faith:

"Will my dog [cat, bird, or hamster] go to heaven?"
"Does my pet have a soul?"
"If they have been so good, why won't they be saved?"
"Will I see them again?"

These questions, for the most part, tackle the crux of faith and belief: *If* there is a God, and *if* that God is a loving God, then what happens to God's creation? Or "If God has made all things, does that mean that all return to their Creator?" And "If our pets live afterward, will we see them again?" Or simply: "What is heaven like?"

So the questions boil down to: Is there a God? If there is a God, then is God a loving God? If God has created everything, does everything created return to its source (God the Creator) after it has died? What is heaven like? In heaven, will we see our loved ones, human and nonhuman, again?

These questions about the nature of God, and about the afterlife, raise questions about core beliefs that I was rarely asked when I was in parish ministry.

> *I trust my beautiful girl Lily is back with the Creator, surrounded by love and that one day I'll be reunited with her.*
>
> —Client

Of course, we cannot answer these questions with certainty. These are mysteries, points of faith, not matters of proof. Yet we can listen to the views of several faith traditions, consider the essence or "spirit" of them, and posit them alongside our own beliefs, hunches, and personal experiences.

Christianity and Judaism

If Martin Luther can speak of a dog's golden tail in the resurrection, in the afterlife, and if the late Rev. Billy Graham can say, "God will prepare everything for our perfect happiness in heaven, and if it takes my dog being there, I believe he'll be there," then questions concerning heaven and the afterlife for our pets deserve to be taken seriously. In the Hebrew Scriptures and Christian Bible, a number of texts can be of comfort:

> *For the fate of humans and the fate of animals is the same; as one dies, so dies the other. They all have the same breath, and humans have no advantage over the animals. . . . All go to one place. (Ecclesiastes 3:19–21)*

> *You save humans and animals alike, O Lord. (Psalm 36:6)*
> *In his hand is the life of every living thing. (Job 12:10)*
> *Are not two sparrows sold for a penny? Yet not one of them will fall to the ground apart from your Father. (Matthew 10:29)*
> *Yet not one of them is forgotten in God's sight. (Luke 12:6b)*
> *For every wild animal of the forest is mine. (Psalm 50:10)*
> *Beloved, let us love one another, because love is from God; everyone who loves is born of God and knows God . . . for God is love. (1 John 4:7,8)*
> *Then I heard every creature in heaven and on earth and under the earth and in the sea, and all that is in them, singing,*
> *"To the one seated on the throne and to the Lamb be blessing and honor and glory and might forever and ever!" (Revelation 5:13)*

Prayers from a number of saints were also imbued with hope. This one, attributed to St. Basil, brings in a scriptural reference (Psalm 36) and is a celebration of the Creator's goodness: "And of these also, O Lord, the humble beasts, who bear with us the heat and burden of the day, we beg you to extend your great kindness of heart, for you promised to save both humans and beasts, and great is your loving kindness."

Yet beside these inspiring and loving words from scripture stands a large stumbling block: the question of the existence of souls in nonhumans. The rationale is that if animals don't have souls, then they will not be admitted to heaven. Lord Byron referred to this notion of animals having no souls in his poem "Epitaph to a Dog," written after the death of his dog, Boatswain:

> *Deny'd in heaven the Soul he held on earth:*
> *While man, vain insect! hopes to be forgiven,*
> *And claims himself a sole exclusive heaven.*

The question "Do animals have souls?" is not a modern one. Theologians have struggled with this issue for hundreds of years. What is the soul? The Hebrew word for soul is *nephesh*, meaning the "breath of life" or "life spark." Let's go to the source of the conflict itself: the animal. The word *animal* comes from the Latin *anima* (breath, spirit, air), so it describes animated, or "ensouled" (endowed with soul, spirit, or breath), beings. To use the word *animal* means to acknowledge that the creature possesses spirit or soul. Part of the problem with the search for an animal's "soul" was due to Western inheritance from the Enlightenment. Descartes thought that animals were mere machines. Humans were granted dominion, placed above the rest of creation. (My understanding of dominion is more along the lines of being a caretaker, and less about dominating or wielding power or control over other species.) For it was believed that humans alone possessed intelligence, could make rational decisions, and had souls. Humankind's "rationality" was seen as being a little below the divine and far superior to that of any animal.

Not everyone thought this way. John Wesley, one of the founders of Methodism, was a vegetarian, and believed that animals had souls. In his journal, he wrote about a visit he made to the Tower of London's menagerie in December 1764, accompanied by a musician friend. Wesley thought that if the animals responded to music, this might decide whether they had souls or not. The animals in question—several lions and a tiger—reacted in a playful manner when the flute was played. Wesley was convinced they moved as they did because they had divine souls within. Wesley continued his reflection in his famous sermon, "The General Deliverance," published in 1781. "What then is the barrier between men and brutes?" wrote Wesley. "The line which they cannot pass? It was not reason. Set aside that ambiguous term: exchange it for the plain word, understanding; and who can deny that brutes have this? We may as well deny that they have sight or hearing."

Not only did Wesley credit animals with possessing reason (or understanding); he believed their former ways of being in the Garden of Eden would change. They will be cared for, made happy by God, and be alive forever. "As there will be nothing within, so there will be nothing without, to give them any uneasiness: No heat or cold, no storm or tempest, but one perennial spring," he wrote. "In the new earth, as well as in the new heavens, there will be nothing to give pain, but everything that the wisdom and goodness of God can create to give happiness . . . when God has 'renewed the face of the earth,' and their corruptible body has put on incorruption, they shall enjoy happiness suited to their state, without alloy, without interruption, and without end."

Victorian fantasy writer and Congregational minister George MacDonald held a position at the Trinity Congregational Church, in the English town of Arundel. One of the reasons he was forced to resign was because he believed that animals went to heaven. This was frowned upon by the congregation, viewed as an unorthodox belief. One congregant wrote, "[F]or it seemed, unbelievably and shockingly, that the young pastor thought that animals would share a place in heaven." In his sermon "Hope of the Gospel," MacDonald wrote these loving words:

*I know of no reason why I should not look for the animals
to rise again, in the same sense in which I hope myself to
rise again—to reappear, clothed with another and better
form of life than before. If the Father will raise his children,
why should he not also raise those whom he has taught his
little ones to love? Love is the one bond of the universe,
the heart of God, the life of his children; if animals can be
loved, they are loveable; if they can love, they are yet more
plainly loveable: love is eternal; how then should its object
perish?*

While some Christians argue that animals possess souls and
will, as a result, obtain eternal life, others disagree. C. S. Lewis's view
diverged from that of his master. While Lewis concluded that there was
animal resurrection, it was conditional; it was only for tame animals
(which seems strange to me, considering Aslan was an "untamed"
lion). Lewis wrote:

*The error we must avoid is that of considering them in
themselves. Man is to be understood only in his relation to
God. The beasts are to be understood only in their relation
to man, and through man, to God. . . . Now it will be
seen that, in so far as the tame animal has a real self or
personality, it owes this almost entirely to its master. If a
good sheepdog seems "almost human" that is because a good
shepherd has made it so . . . you must not think of a beast by
itself, and call that a personality and then inquire whether
God will raise and bless that . . . it seems to me possible that
certain animals may have an immortality, not in themselves,
but in the immortality of their masters.*

Lewis's argument concerning an afterlife for pets seems to rest solely on the state of the pet's human owner, rather than on the animal itself.

Within some more current Protestant circles, guidelines to beliefs and teachings about animals are spelled out. The United Methodist website advocates caring for animals and supporting humane treatment of them, yet states: "We United Methodists do not teach that animals have souls and therefore need redemption and forgiveness or heaven in the same way that humans do." This teaching appears to be reflected in a blog by Rev. Dr. Frederick W. Schmidt Jr. In his blogpost "All Dogs Go to Heaven," Schmidt writes of eternity, of the new heaven and new earth, saying he could not envisage such a place without animals in it. He goes on to say that we can imagine such a place, without having to think that our pets are like us or that they have souls. He writes that we are not the same. There are differences, because "dogs do not have souls, nor are they made in the image of God, but to coin a phrase, 'All dogs go to heaven.'" My reading of this is that, according to Schmidt, animals may be part of this new eternal vision, however it unfolds, but only humans have immortal souls.

This argument is ongoing, still debated by some clergy and laypeople. I remember receiving a phone call from a distressed client. Her daughter, who attended a Catholic school, had requested a prayer to be said for her dying rabbit and was told in no uncertain terms by her teacher that rabbits did not have souls so they wouldn't pray for it. Needless to say, the child was grief stricken, as was her mother. I couldn't help but wonder what implications this action might have on their faith or on their willingness to attend church.

> *I truly hope one day to see my many friends that have passed over before me, and I told Cloud we would see each other again. Most people think I'm crazy and*

animals don't have souls. I would like to think that
they do. They hold no grudges. Cloud never let her
nasty start to her life get in the way of being a very
kind and giving dog, toward people and other animals.
She truly showed that out of horrible circumstances
could come forgiveness and rising above all hurt and
enjoy her life and it showed in everything she did. I'm
so proud of her for that.

—Client

So Do All Dogs Go to Heaven?

In December 2014, many Catholics became quite excited when it was reported that Pope Francis had pronounced that animals go to heaven. The Italian newspaper *Corriere della Sera* discussed the pope's remarks, which had been made during a general audience in November and concluded that animals have a place in heaven. This positive announcement turned out to be a misquote, a misinterpretation, a mistranslation. According to Vatican Radio, the pope had said, "The Holy Scripture teaches us that the fulfillment of this wonderful design also affects everything around us." Pope Francis had been speaking of a new earth and a new creation, but he did not say that animals have an afterlife. The animal-friendly words Pope Francis was quoted as saying—"One day, we will see our animals again in the eternity of Christ. Paradise is open to all of God's creatures"—had *not* been proclaimed by Pope Francis. They had been spoken by a previous pope, Pope Paul VI, in a pastoral context to comfort a grieving boy whose dog had died. This misreporting had gathered momentum due to social media and people's longing that it be true. It had featured on the front page of the *New York Times*, as well as other reputable newspapers. Such a statement may have been in keeping with Pope Francis's stance on creation, so it is easy to see how this mistake or assumption had been made.

In Christianity, there are differences of opinion concerning pets going to heaven after they die. For many Protestants—including theologians such as animal theologian Rev. Professor Andrew Linzey, founding director of the Oxford Centre for Animal Ethics, and Rev. Gary Kowalski, author of a number of books, including *The Souls of Animals* and *Goodbye, Friend*—it involves a personal belief in God and the integrity and high status and value of animals, with or without souls. In Catholicism, theological or doctrinal matters are usually decreed by church hierarchy, but individuals also hold personal views about these issues, including the late Friar Jack Wintz, who wrote *I Will See You in Heaven.*

In conclusion, perhaps Protestants and Catholics hear what is needed during a pastoral encounter. Were Luther's words about the dog obtaining a "golden tail" and Pope Paul VI's remarks to a grieving dog owner theological arguments or pastoral utterances—statements said in order to provide comfort?

In Judaism there isn't a clear, definitive answer either. For the most part, mainstream Judaism does not believe that animals have immortal souls. Although in the mystical Kabbalah, there is a belief in transmigration of the soul, that soul is thought to be of a human, a soul that may be trapped in an animal's body, for a specific reason (such as certain work to be completed). Judaism is a religion that focuses on the now rather than the afterlife, so it is understandable that the answer to the question "Will my dog go to heaven?" is either "No" (for if there is anything after we die, it will be reserved for humans) or "We don't know."

Of course, if one is consulting Scripture for clear answers, they will not be found, because the keeping of pets is not mentioned in

Scripture. The care of work animals and livestock is addressed. We learn that, if in your employ, they are to be cared for, and they are to be fed before you. (As a young child, my mother would say, "Remember, our pets cannot open the refrigerator. We feed them before ourselves.") In the Talmud, it is stated that you may not purchase an animal unless you are able to feed it. "Rabbi Eleazar . . . explained: nobody is permitted to buy domesticated or wild animals or birds unless he has food prepared for them." Nowadays, this would also apply to pets.

Jewish Mourning Rituals for Animals

In Judaism animals are to be cared for, as they have been created by God, but the concept of an afterlife, or of animals having souls, is not part of mainstream thinking. There is some disagreement though, concerning rituals and prayers that are permitted to be recited after the death of a pet. "[I]t is not appropriate to incorporate our traditional mourning/memorial liturgy (i.e. Eil Male Rachamim and Kaddish) for this purpose," writes one rabbi. "Although we love and adore our pets . . . they are not human. It is important that we remain cognizant of the boundaries that do exist as a part of the natural world . . . honoring our creature companions without debasing the responsibilities, benefits and privileges that come with being human."

Consensus seems to be that animals have been made lower than human beings, and therefore, funeral rites and observances that pertain to humans do not apply to nonhumans. On a number of websites, there are several heartrending stories about persons wishing to observe key rituals for their pets, but being told that those rituals and practices are solely for humans, and are not to be held, or recited, for animals.

One of the key rituals for mourners is the desire to say Kaddish (the mourner's prayer) for their deceased pets. The Kaddish (Hebrew for "holy") praises God, but does not speak of death. It is said after the death of close relatives, and is recited daily for eleven months, usually at a synagogue where a minyan, a quorum of ten adults, is present, to signify that no mourner is alone in their grief. Minimum requirements concerning numbers needed, as well as the subject of whether women are permitted to recite the Kaddish, differ within denominations. Several stories online speak of how their pet (usually a dog or a cat) was definitely a member of the family, and therefore deserving of respect and remembrance. For some, this includes a yearning to recite the Kaddish.

Another ritual discussed is that of sitting Shiva, which is a seven-day mourning period, observed after the death of a close relative. This is time set apart from ordinary daily living, to aid spiritual and emotional healing. During the week people come to visit and provide care for the mourners. I know that some Jews have wondered whether they may sit Shiva for their pet. I remember meeting a Jewish colleague who introduced me to one of her colleagues. When her colleague discovered that I was a chaplain at an animal hospital, she told me that she had just finished sitting Shiva for her deceased pet.

Another prayer that is said when someone has died is "Baruch dayan ha'emet," or "Blessed is the True Judge." According to Orthodox rabbi Ari Enkin, it is not appropriate to recite this after an animal has died, the only allowance being made for a human experiencing financial loss on the death of the animal. A modern example would be praying it following the death of a therapy dog.

Online, these mourning practices have been discussed by rabbis from a number of traditions. Some counsel against the saying of the Kaddish or sitting Shiva, saying these are not suitable rites for nonhumans, whereas others suggest a rewording of the Kaddish. This seems harsh, yet even rabbis who feel unable to support the concept of drawing on Jewish resources for mourning animal companions suggest praying prayers, thanking God for pets, and for the joy they have brought the person. It appears that the Reformed, Liberal, and Conservative traditions are more open to the idea of accommodating the mourners than the Orthodox or Ultra-Orthodox traditions. This may be due, in part, to a lower number of Orthodox or Ultra-Orthodox members having pets.

If the Jewish mourner is forbidden to recite a prayer said to be reserved for humans only, and they do not wish to do something deemed wrong in their tradition, then I would suggest that they pray a different prayer or sit on their own or with their family, share stories about their deceased pet, give thanks to God for that precious gift, and ask God to continue to look after their animal companion.

What about euthanasia? In Judaism, euthanasia is acceptable in order to end suffering and ongoing pain, so euthanizing on compassionate grounds is permissible. Having said that, in Judaism as in Christianity, many would prefer their pet to die a natural death, so one does not have to make the decision to euthanize. Often the decision is accompanied by a feeling of fear and guilt that you are taking a life—playing God, if you will. The sacredness of life hits one in the face when that hard matter concerning the ending of a loved one's life has to be made or faced.

Rabbi Jonathan Wittenberg, of the New North London Synagogue, cofounder of Eco-Synagogue, and senior rabbi of Masorti Judaism (traditional, nonfundamentalist Judaism) in the UK, wrote a book about his two dogs, Safi and Mitzpah. In Wittenberg's book, *Things My Dog Has Taught Me About Being a Better Human*, he tells of the dreadful day when he took his elderly dog Safi to the vet to be put to sleep. He knew it was the right decision, the kindest decision—but oh, so hard. Before the injection was given, they gathered around Safi.

"We prayed for him, because every individual life is part of the sacred bond of all life," he writes. "I carefully put my hand over his eyes, as is the custom to avoid distraction when reciting the Shema meditation, in which the oneness of God in all things is proclaimed." The vet proceeded to administer the injection, "gently helping him to his place in the world to come."

Does Wittenberg believe there is an afterlife for dogs? He appears to be open to the possibility: "I, too, can't imagine heaven, if heaven really is a physical abode, in which dogs are not there. If God is love, and present in all the love there is, then surely dogs must belong with God, and where else is that but heaven?"

I wonder if Wittenberg's views arose out of his passion for creation? His convictions, or hopes, seem at the opposite end of the spectrum from other, more conservative perspectives in Judaism.

Islamic Views About Animals and Pets

"All the beasts that roam the earth and all the birds that soar on high are but communities like your own," we read in Qur'an 6:38. In Islam, animals are mentioned in three main sources: the Qur'an (revealed scripture), the Hadith (reports about the words and deeds of the Prophet Muhammad), and the sharia (Islamic law). There is no unified Islamic view of nonhuman animals, so attitudes and behavior may vary within different cultures and regions.

In Islam, animals are referred to as communities. Indeed, they are acknowledged as followers who submit to God's laws, and thus are Muslim. Animals, as believers, are spiritual in nature. According to an English translation of Qur'an 16:49, animals glorify, praise, and worship God: "To God bow all creatures of the heavens and the earth. . . . They are not disdainful; they fear their Lord on high and do as they are bidden." Each creature is made for itself and in order to praise its Creator. Islam (or "submission") is an ideal understood by believers as the state God wills for his creation. In the Qur'an, everything God/Allah has created submits to his will.

The Islamic view of the world is a hierarchical one, with the human community occupying a higher rank than all other animal communities. This is also reflected in the matter of the soul. Animals have animal souls, which differ from human souls, which are rational. This means that humans alone face judgment, which may include admittance to paradise. Animals are not subject to judgment, and therefore are not recipients of an afterlife. The majority of Muslims would say that animals do not have an afterlife, a belief that at times has been challenged.

Some Mu'tazilites, who were a school of Islamic theologians prominent in the ninth century, thought that if animals were well-behaved—that is, "good"—then they would, like humans, enjoy life in heaven, whereas nasty animals would follow the fate of evil humans, residing in hell. One Mu'tazilite theologian, Abu Ishaq an-Nazzam (c. 775–c. 845), held even more radical views: he believed all animals would go to heaven.

The afterlife of animals continued to be discussed among some Qur'an commentators. One, Muhammad ibn Jarir-al-Tabari (839–923), stated that animals "have knowledge in the way you (human beings) have knowledge, manage their lives in the way you do, and their good and bad deeds are preserved in the Mother of the Book (the same way yours are). Then, God . . . will resurrect them, and will compensate them for their deeds and their misdeeds on the Judgement Day."

The Qur'anic verse, "No creature is there crawling on the earth, no bird flying with its wings, but they are like nations to you. We have neglected nothing in the Book; then to their Lord they shall be mustered" (Qur'an 6:38), has been interpreted to indicate resurrection for all life, as well as compensation for any suffering or injustice experienced during an animal's earthly life.

Although there is no consensus in Islam concerning whether animals enter the afterlife, it is worth noting that pet ownership is not large among Muslims, so the question of deceased pets going to paradise after they die may not be often asked. Part of the reason pet ownership is low is that dogs do not reside in many households as pets. They may be used as guard dogs, or as hunting dogs, but they are not kept as pets. This is due to a number of Hadiths, which have reservations regarding dogs. Some of these may be cultural rather than religious reasons, and many are positions that are being challenged today. Cats, on the other hand, have been embraced (literally and metaphorically) by many Muslims, one reason being because they were loved by Muhammad. One story tells of Muhammad cutting around his good robe, so as not to disturb his cat, Meuzza, who was sleeping on it. The "M," which can be seen on tabby cats, is said to be from a blessing given by Muhammad. Cats are viewed as being ritually clean, therefore permitted to enter homes and mosques.

Reincarnation and Rebirth

In religions that assent to reincarnation or rebirth, the question of "Is there a heaven?" doesn't apply. Rather, the question is more along the lines of "What will happen to my pet's energy or consciousness following its physical death?"

Hinduism
Hindus believe that both animals and humans contain souls, and all souls form part of the supreme soul. This means that animal souls are

not regarded as inferior, but equal to those of humans. After animals and humans die, they experience rebirth in either animal or human form. Karma is a major factor in determining whether a soul is born in a human body, or in an animal life-form. It is believed that one must undergo many rebirths before attaining human form, and it is only as a human that one is allowed entry to heaven, or to attain what is known as *moksha* (release from *samsara*, which is the cycle of death and rebirth). It is thought that animals, though equal in spiritual status, are not gifted with being able to make rational decisions or intelligent choices, so they need to be rebirthed as a human in order to achieve liberation.

In the Vedic tradition, a human has two births, the first within an animal body. He or she remains as an animal until he or she has been initiated into spiritual knowledge, which then heralds a second birth, in the form of a human. So even though the animal soul is not inferior to that of a human soul, being housed in a human body is necessary for reaching release or liberation.

There are myths and legends from Hindu scriptures, including from the Puranas, that tell of animals expressing their devotion to a higher being. It is worth noting that during several of Vishnu's incarnations (when he assumed different avatars), a number of these were in animal form, including a fish, a tortoise, and a boar.

In Hinduism, there is some uncertainty regarding what happens to the animal soul after physical death, whether the soul continues to exist, whether it resides in the same ancestral place as humans, or whether it ends up somewhere quite different.

Buddhism

In Buddhism there isn't an ending, or an afterlife, per se. Death is viewed as a transition, our earthly life leading to rebirth or reincarnation.

Although in Buddhism human birth is considered superior, because only humans can achieve nirvana, various Buddhist texts remind us that people were once animals and can take on animal form. There are a number of stories about animals who perform virtuous acts and by doing so ensure for themselves either heavenly or human birth. All forms of Buddhism emphasize the principles of loving kindness, compassion, and *ahimsa* (nonviolence/non-injury), and follow the Noble Eightfold Path. In Buddhism there are no commandments, so adherents live out their lives as they see fit as they follow "the Way."

Buddhism views nonhuman beings as fellow beings, leading to some guidelines and sensitivity regarded ailing pets, euthanasia, care of the body, and the animal's consciousness. In Buddhism it is accepted that animals have consciousness, and that after their physical bodies and brains have shut down, the mind will move on to different experiences or states.

According to Buddhist writer David Michie, euthanasia is not encouraged. He prefers a natural death process, rather than what could be a rushed, frantic euthanasia. Michie's concern stems from the concept of karma and karmic implications. How animals transition from this life to the next is best prepared for with quiet. This allows them to complete what they have to do, rather than deal with sudden interruptions that may lead to karmic repercussions. Karma and how one's consciousness transitions are key. Michie advocates natural death because it allows the animal (and the human) to mentally prepare for the next stage, to be conscious of the process, to accept what is happening, and then to prepare for it. This can be undertaken as good palliative care. Michie writes that if it is karma for the pet to experience pain, pain killers can help, but if euthanasia was to take place, then that animal might keep experiencing pain during the intermediate, or "bardo," state that could have been avoided. "What is the karmic impact of our pet dying prematurely—from their side—without understanding the enormity of what's happening?" writes Michie. "How will they cope with an abrupt physical and mental dissolution without notice? We are hardly helping them make the best of this critical transition."

If euthanasia needs to take place, then it is preferable for it to be performed at home, in a quiet environment, surrounded by loved ones, with mantras and chants being said.

In addition to physical dissolution, mental dissolution also takes place, which involves a number of stages. In Buddhism there is an understanding that following death (for both humans and animals), subtle consciousness can remain for a period of time. This bardo state is the in-between time: between the lifetime that has ended and the one that is to come, the "rebirth." It is believed that bardo can last a few moments or up to seven weeks. This belief dictates matters concerning care of the deceased's body, personal surroundings, and observances during this seven-week period.

The state of mind during this time of transition is important. It may affect or determine events in the future, regarding rebirth. Embodiment can still be influenced during these forty-nine days, thoughts and feelings being of paramount importance. This is one reason why it is important to try to give much-loved pets a gentle or peaceful death. If possible, the body is left undisturbed, perhaps draped in flowers, or surrounded by candles.

According to Michie, nothing is fixed or certain during the bardo state. It is the time when the person or animal starts to take on the form for its rebirth (as human or animal). Feelings and energies are intensified. It is thought that if we think about something during this state, such as our old home, we can be there, perhaps as in a dream. For some Buddhists, this informs how they handle the deceased one's belongings.

If a human, their place at the table is still set, in case they visit. If they were to visit and those items were not in place, they might feel they have been forgotten. For pets, Michie suggests that their belongings, including their beds, toys, food, and water bowls, be left out.

During the bardo state, the deceased, moving forward to rebirth, can still be influenced by generous and loving acts, such as acts of compassion for others, or through charitable donations. During this seven-week period, each week, on the anniversary of the day of the death, the bardo state undergoes a mini-death, which signals that rebirth is not fixed, it may change form. What happens now can affect the future, so it is important to be generous, positive, calm, and loving, and to recite prayers and mantras for the pet's well-being. By the forty-ninth day after death, rebirth will have taken place. Buddhists suggest that this is the time to accept that the deceased, in the form of consciousness, has moved on to a new experience.

Helping Children Understand

How do we speak of such beliefs, in relation to deceased animal companions, with children? One children's picture book, *Samsara Dog* by Helen Manos, addresses this issue, from the point of view of Buddhism. The book tells of Samsara Dog (*samsara* being the cycle of death and rebirth), a dog who lived many lives, until the last one, in which he gave his human companion the gifts of hope, comfort, and great love. Compassion placed Samsara Dog on the path to nirvana. He was released from the cycle of death and rebirth, so he didn't come back again.

In the Indian epic, the *Mahabharata*, there is a story about the emperor Yudhishthira, who, at the end of his reign, travels to the Himalayas, accompanied by his wife and his four brothers. A small pariah dog attaches himself to the group. Along the way, all of the royal troupe dies, with the exception of Yudhishthira and the dog. Eventually they come to the end of the journey, arriving at the gates of heaven, where they are met by Indra and invited to join him in his chariot for the trip into heaven.

Yudhishthira replies, "This dog, O Lord of the Past and the Present, has been a constant and faithful companion to me. He should go with me. My heart is full of compassion for him."

Indra says to leave the dog. Yudhishthira pleads again, speaking of the dog's devotion. Indra throws him a counterargument, saying that there is no place in heaven for people with dogs, and in fact, there are deities who strip such persons of their merits.

Yudhishthira pleads again, stating that he will not abandon a creature to achieve his own personal happiness. Indra, the king of the gods, tries one more time, telling Yudhishthira in no uncertain terms that if he abandons the dog, he will earn the reward of heaven. Besides, he has already abandoned everything else, given up his brothers and his wife, so why not a dog? Yudhishthira still refuses to give in to Indra's request, saying that he had abandoned those who were dead, but this dog is alive. At this point, the dog reveals himself to be none other than Dharma, the god of righteousness. In a version by Jean Houston, the king announces:

> *"Paradise won't be paradise for me if the only way I get in is by abandoning an animal who has been good to me. Shut the gates. We'll stay out here together."*
>
> *"Come in! Come in!" cried the gatekeeper. "You have been faithful to the end and so has your dog. Your dog is a living example of the dharma, the way of truth. He has been with you always. Come in. Come in."*
>
> *And the great king and his dog entered Paradise.*

The Rainbow Bridge

It is important that those who do not profess an adherence to an established religion but who state that they are spiritual are not overlooked. (I often say that not everyone is *religious*, but all are *spiritual* beings.) The death of a loved one, in this case an animal companion, can be a crippling time. Various poems and sayings have been of help to many, including those who admit that they have religious affiliation and follow a particular belief system. While these writings would not be classified as scripture or sacred texts, they serve a similar purpose: comforting those who mourn.

> *It [The Rainbow Bridge poem] gave me such peace and comfort in my time of grief, I have framed the poem with a photo of Pete, and although I am still grieving for Pete, I need only to look at the photo and poem and I feel a sense of peace and calm. I pray for Pete and all the other pets who have left us and truly hope that they are at Rainbow Bridge.*
>
> —Client

One of the best known, if not *the* best known, poems about an afterlife for pets is a reflection known as "The Rainbow Bridge." There are different variants, signifying that it has an ongoing life of its own. Here is one version, by an unknown author:

> *Just this side of heaven is a place called Rainbow Bridge. When an animal dies that has been especially close to someone here, that pet goes to Rainbow Bridge. There are meadows and hills for all of our special friends so they can run and play together. There is plenty of food, water, and*

sunshine, and our friends are warm and comfortable. All the animals who had been ill and old are restored to health and vigor. Those who were hurt or maimed are made whole and strong again, just as we remember them in our dreams of days and times gone by. The animals are happy and content, except for one small thing; they each miss someone very special to them, who had to be left behind. They all run and play together, but the day comes when one suddenly stops and looks into the distance. His bright eyes are intent. His eager body quivers. Suddenly he begins to run from the group, flying over the green grass, his legs carrying him faster and faster. You have been spotted, and when you and your special friend finally meet, you cling together in joyous reunion, never to be parted again. The happy kisses rain upon your face; your hands again caress the beloved head, and you look once more into the trusting eyes of your pet, so long gone from your life but never absent from your heart. Then you cross Rainbow Bridge together.

There is uncertainty concerning the authorship of "The Rainbow Bridge." There are a number of versions, including one, penned by Steve and Diane Bodofsky, that is in rhyme. In any case, these words have brought great comfort to thousands of grieving pet owners. Like "Footprints" or "Footprints in the Sand," a reflection about Christ carrying one during times of anxiety and grief, the authorship may be contested, but that does not diminish the comfort these words have brought to many readers.

The Rainbow Bridge is affixed to the wall in many veterinarian practices. Sometimes the reflection is given out, emailed, or mailed to the owner after their pet has been euthanized or has died following surgery or an illness.

In the story, pastures or meadows are described as part of the landscape in the afterlife for animals. Many Canadians are familiar with the book *Beautiful Joe*, written by Canadian author Margaret Marshall Saunders in 1893 to highlight animal cruelty (it served a similar function to that of Anna Sewell's *Black Beauty*, written in 1877). Saunders wrote a sequel, *Beautiful Joe's Paradise, or the Island of Brotherly Love* (1902), which described an afterlife for pets, complete with meadows. The trip was not via a rainbow bridge but courtesy of a balloon. When we consider that it was written in 1902 and speaks of a heaven or land for deceased animals, we see how radical and controversial its theological ideas would have been at the time. Saunders was the daughter of a Baptist minister. In the preface to the book, Saunders writes about having discussed writing a book about a paradise for animals with her father, who encouraged her to do so. The topic of animals having souls is brought up in the first few pages:

> *"Do dogs go to heaven?" I asked.*
> *She was quite shocked. . . . She said she didn't know—*
> *she would ask her clergyman, but she thought that*
> *when animals died they just turned to earth.*
> *"But there was something alive inside Ragtime,*
> *Mother," I argued, "something that would never die."*

Later, the boy in Saunders's story sees the transformation:

> *I caught my breath. There was another Ragtime lying dead*
> *on the balcony, the very image of my own Ragtime, but*
> *I held on to the real one.*
> *"This dog has his spirit in him," said the old monkey, softly;*
> *"you must not bury him."*

I caught hold of his hairy old arm again. "Will he come to
*   life?"*
He nodded.
"And be just as he was here?"
"Exactly."
Something choked me. "Where?" I said.
"On the Island of Brotherly Love."

On this island, which is one of several, the last one being the final
World of the Blessed, animals that were mutilated or injured on earth
are fully restored, made new or whole. What a fine vision!

Some have hypothesized that the Rainbow Bridge is based on the
Bifröst, or Bilröst, the burning rainbow bridge in Norse mythology that
reaches between Midgard (Earth, the human realm) and Asgard, the
realm of the Aesir, the Nordic gods. In Norse mythology, everything
known about the Bifröst comes from thirteenth-century literature. The
rainbow bridge was described as the "best of bridges" and is extremely
strong, having been built by the skills and magic of the gods themselves. The gods rode their horses across the Bifröst bridge every day to
reach the holy well, where the gods held court. The bridge also trans-
ported the souls of men who had proved worthy as warriors.

Whatever the origins or the melding of traditions, legends, and
authors, the Rainbow Bridge story has certainly brought comfort to
many grieving pet owners.

After-Death Mysteries

What of the more esoteric, or New Age, beliefs? What of those bereaved
owners who have a more obvious psychic bent or belief? Some of these
beliefs contain similar concepts found within traditional religions, or

at least, held by bereaved pet owners who adhere to a traditional or mainstream religion.

I have had clients speak of feeling their deceased animal on their bed or hearing the sound of paws on wooden floors. Some speak of seeing their animal flash past their eyes for a second or of hearing the meow or howl of their cat or dog. These admissions—often accompanied by "I might be going mad, but . . ." or "You will think I am bonkers . . ."—are aired by rational individuals. Many times I was the only person, or the first person, in whom the bereaved owner had confided this. These noises, and other sensory experiences, are often interpreted as a means of comfort, perhaps a message for the bereaved from their deceased animal companion, letting them know that they are at peace, and safe, and that their energy and love will always surround or accompany their human friend in some way. These can be termed types of "after-death communication."

According to veterinarian, author, and animal advocate Dr. Michael W. Fox, these are quite common. He says: "Some human-attached animals seem to be able to will themselves to be with their beloved human companions after they have died. . . . An overarching aspect of all the letters I have received on this subject of animals' spirits is this unifying, space-time transcending emotional element that we call love."

There are many mysteries that can never be proven or solved. Hearing, seeing, feeling, or even smelling one's old dog or cat should not be dismissed or pushed aside as "Oh, I am just too emotional," "I am just imagining it," or "Maybe I am dehydrated (or anemic or sleep deprived)." Whenever a client told me a story that contained this type of mysterious element—usually told with much hesitancy ("What will the minister think?")—I would ask myself: *Does this comfort the mourner? Is it a healthy way to think?* If I could answer yes to both questions, then I took that sensory or auditory visit as a gift, a source of comfort.

There is some commonality between certain psychic beliefs and traditional religious beliefs. Both seek to comfort, to reassure, to strengthen. I am not psychic or telepathic. Some psychics have written books about what happens to our pets in the afterlife and about continuing communication between the deceased pet and their owner. Although psychic or telepathic communication lies outside my area of expertise, these accounts may be helpful for some readers.

I cannot answer, with absolute certainty, the question of what happens after death to animals (or to humans), but I can say that I believe in a loving Creator who will continue to care for creation and that, in my tradition, there is the assurance of an afterlife.

Similarly, many wonder about deceased pets being seen or felt in near-death experiences. Although there is no systematic record of accounts of pets greeting humans who have undergone near-death experiences, people who have had near-death experiences do sometimes recount stories of being greeted by former pets or pets who belonged to other family members, such as grandparents. One such account goes like this: "As I raised my head up from the ground to look around, I saw my deceased dog from my childhood bounding towards me. . . . It was overwhelmingly wonderful. I felt completely at peace and totally happy. I was so excited to see her again, and I did not question the experience at the time."

This is not surprising; the bonds are strong. Why wouldn't pets be seen? In cases concerning terminally ill children who have a near-death dream or vision, some mention that they have dreamed of, or been visited by, their deceased pet. The frequency of pets—rather than humans—greeting them may be because they don't know any close relatives who have died, whereas their pet, who was a member of their family, perhaps even their best friend, in many cases an animal who was deeply loved, they can recognize and name. Near-death experiences cannot be proven, but what can be shown are that the results are transformative. The sight or feel of a beloved deceased pet comforts the ill, and decreases their fear of dying and death.

There are said to be "thin" places in the world, many of these locations becoming sites of pilgrimage. These physical places, thought to be located at the edges between the earthly and heavenly realms, are porous or transparent. They include places such as the Scottish island of Iona and Glastonbury. Perhaps grieving opens up the spiritual realm in a different way? When one grieves, prayers, tears, and hopes about what exists beyond the earthly are at the forefront. Sometimes people mention being visited by the Holy or feeling God's presence at a sad time in their life. Perhaps when we are grieving, at our lowest, we are given comfort and the assurance that love continues. Perhaps when we grieve, we inhabit a "thin" place.

HEARTBEAT

How pleasant to know Mr Lear! . . .
He has many friends, laymen and clerical;
Old Foss is the name of his cat . . .
His body is perfectly spherical . . .

—Edward Lear

WRITER AND ARTIST Edward Lear, known for his nonsense verse, loved his cat, Foss. Lear had obtained a cat he called Potiphar, but that feline went missing. Potiphar had a brother, who was given to Lear after Potiphar's misadventure. Lear named him Adelphos (Greek for "brother"), shortening it to Foss.

Foss's tail was short—only half a tail, in fact. Foss's tail had been docked to keep him from wandering like his now-absent brother. This was due to a superstition, held in some parts of Greece, that a cat will not wander from its home if the other part of its tail remains there.

Lear's devotion to Foss could be seen in the lengths he went to when they moved to a new villa in San Remo. Lear's new building was modeled on the old one, so that Foss would not be confused when they moved to the new home.

An aside: It should come as no surprise that Lear is best remembered for penning the marvelous "The Owl and the Pussycat." That cat gained immortality, but the cat was not Foss. The poem was written in 1871, a year before Foss took up residence with Lear.

Now Foss, like most cats, was not perfect. At one time Lear banished Foss to the kitchen because the cat had developed a habit of ripping up letters. Soon, though, as is usually the way with cats, all was forgiven. Foss became much loved, "a good addition to one's lonely, lonely, life," wrote Lear.

Lear enjoyed drawing Foss. Foss adorned many of Lear's letters, as well as serving as the model for some of his finest caricatures, including being the "C" in Lear's alphabet series. Lear even designed a coat of arms for Foss and drew the exquisite nonsense *Foss Couchant*, *Foss Rampant*, *Foss Dansant*, and *Foss, "a untin."*

As Foss aged, he became quite rotund; at one stage he had trouble getting through a doorway. His large girth is beautifully drawn by Lear; indeed, the largeness of his belly seems to reflect that of his owner. Cat and writer-illustrator merge and blend, even down to the enormous round eyes of Foss, which resemble Lear's bespectacled ones.

We only have Lear's drawings as a permanent reminder of this feline's looks. Lear and Foss were at a sitting, ready to be photographed together, but just before the photograph was taken, Foss jumped down, Lear's hand still in position around the absent cat. If you didn't know what had happened, you might think it was just a lovely photograph of Lear. This was the last photograph of the man fondly remembered as the greatest writer, and father, of nonsense verse.

Lear's last letter, written on November 29, 1887, speaks of the death of dear Foss: "Foss is dead: & I am glad to say did not suffer at all-having become quite paralyzed on all one side of him. So he was placed in a box yesterday, & buried deep below the Figtree at the end of the Orange walk & tomorrow there will be a stone placed giving the date of his death & his age (31 years,)—(of which 30 were passed in my house)."

Dear Lear, he didn't get the mathematics right! Maybe it was wishful thinking. Foss came to live with Lear when he was several years old, but Foss was hardly thirty-one years of age when he died. Seventeen was more accurate. Yet the error remained, with too many years inscribed in Italian on Foss's elaborate tombstone:

> *Qui sotto sta seppolito il mio buon*
> *Gatto Foss. Era 30 anni in casa mia,*
> *e morì il 26 November 1887—in età*
> *31 anni.*

> Translation: *Beneath this stone was buried*
> *my good cat Foss. He was 30 years in my house,*
> *and died on 26 November 1887—at*
> *31 years of age.*

Lear had him buried in the garden under the fig tree near the terrace, at the Villa Tennyson.

In Lear's final letter, he wrote about the depth of his grief: "All those friends who have known my life will understand that I grieve over this loss." Lear never recovered from the loss of his dear feline companion, and loneliness set in. Two months later, Lear followed the way of his cat, dying on January 29, 1888. More people attended Foss's funeral than Lear's.

3

YOUNG HEARTS

Children and the Loss of an Animal Companion

THE DEATH OF a pet can be a child's first experience of death, so it's vital that this event is approached sensitively and taken seriously.

Having said that, it is important to honor pet death on its own terms and not view or talk about it as preparation for human (or "real") death. Sadly, these sentiments are still voiced today. They do not lessen the grief, and they do not help! We grieve for the ones we love, and the death of a pet is not a "lesson" to strengthen us for human death. It may, of course, help prepare children for the facts of life and death, but it should not be viewed as a lesser or preparatory death. We never know the depths of a bond, for children or for adults.

I grew up in a family whose members included treasured pets, and I remember the death of each and every one of them. I grieved deeply and still miss them. I do not remember being told their deaths were preparation for human loss. When my grandparents died, I do not think the deaths of several pets helped me at all. All loss, all death, is individual, unique.

If pets are seen as family, as integral members of the family unit, then loss will be part of the experience for child and adult. Of course, the death of an animal companion can be the appropriate time to speak about the life cycle, but I believe a pet's death should never be "weighed" or deemed less important than that of a human. That sets one up for carrying around the grief scales. As parents or caregivers, we need to stand back a little, for no one knows the bond between any living being and another except for the parties directly involved. What may appear to be "just a dog" could have been that child's best friend, confidante, cheerleader, therapy dog, or sibling.

It can be quite emotional for parents to talk to their children after the death of the family pet, or as the pet deteriorates, with death imminent. Some of the difficulty is because of the emotions that rise to the surface; not everyone is comfortable crying in front of their children. In this case, I would say it is usually helpful for children to know that the death of their pet has upset their parents too, that they loved the animal. It is a time for free conversation, to acknowledge hard feelings, to even talk about mystery.

Remember, these conversations can touch on eternal questions (such as "Is there a heaven?") and may make you think or rethink your own thoughts and beliefs. It is natural as parents to try to protect our children from being hurt, but, in this case, such protection can make it harder as the child gets older. I grew up at a time when children were not welcome at funerals. I found that difficult, being unable to say farewell to my grandparents. Welcoming children and teenagers to funerals and memorial services has been a great move forward. It is about openness, grieving together, noting that individuals grieve differently, and, hopefully, having some support during the coming days.

At different ages, children think differently. It is helpful to know a little of these stages because they can ease the path through grief. I am not a psychotherapist or a psychologist; I come to this topic as a member of the clergy, with training in pastoral care and basic counseling. For more detailed information about children and pet loss, particularly relating to different age groups, please see Wallace Sife's *The Loss of a Pet* and Cheri Barton Ross's *Pet Loss and Children*. Both are excellent resources for parents and caregivers.

When the child is young, in the two-to-three-year-old bracket, the child has no understanding of death but will see your emotions— your tears—and may be upset by them. It is important to let them know that their pet has died and will not be coming back, but that it is no one's fault; it is part of life. This is probably enough of an explanation for this age group.

For four-to-six-year-olds, the experience may be different and can be built on. The child may have some understanding of death but may not understand that this means "forever." If they see their deceased pet, they may think the animal is asleep and will wake up later, or is playing a game, like "playing dead." Watch how you phrase your explanation if the pet died because of illness or age. Children become ill, as do their parents and relatives and friends, and aging happens. Make sure your child does not equate sickness with death or aging with death. Again, it is important to stress that their pet's death was not due to anything they did or didn't do; death is part of life. Reassure them. Monitor their sleep patterns. If they are reluctant to go to bed, you may need to explore what it means to say that a pet has been "put to sleep," reassuring them this doesn't mean that when they go to sleep, they die. Watch for nightmares. Sometimes drawing a picture of their pet helps with expressing emotions. Offer questions or prompts like "What was funny about Boris?" or "The thing I loved most about Boris was . . ." Stress that these memories remain in their hearts. If having a photo of their deceased pet next to their bed would be comforting, set that up. It might be an opportunity for them to say "Good night, Boris" as they get into bed.

Concrete thinking can make dealing with death a little shocking for older family members. A child may be quite matter of fact about the death, seem to accept it, and even ask in the next day or two when they are getting another dog or cat. These can be trying times for others in the family, who are also grieving and perhaps feeling that their heart will never mend. It is important to point out to other children in the household that this sibling is not trying to be insensitive or uncaring. This is how they cope with abstract concepts such as death, at this age or stage in their development.

For seven-to-ten-year-olds, this is a time when some will have experienced human death in the family (and maybe animal death as well). Some of their questions may be quite difficult to hear, let alone answer. It is important to let their teachers know about the death, so that the teacher can keep track of their behavior at school, noting anything that seems out of character. These days, many schools have classroom pets, so it is possible that the subject of pet loss may already have been discussed in class.

It is important to note that children (and adults) may grieve quite differently from others, including their friends or family members. Ten-to-eleven-year-olds and adolescents may grieve in ways similar to adults, knowing that death happens to every living thing and that in most cases it wasn't due to something they had done or hadn't done. (Accidents do happen, though.) Sometimes teenagers may appear to be "cool" about the death, even appear to be unconcerned, but of course that can be a cover, a protective shield. If their friends have pets or were familiar with the deceased pet, then feelings might be aired and thereby addressed in a safe, secure environment.

Processing the Loss

Pets can be a constant through other, difficult losses, including divorce, moving house, the death of a parent or sibling, moving schools, the loss of a friendship. When the pet dies this lifeline, our four-legged (or multi-feathered or -finned) support system has too.

When we grieve, the intensity of feelings can overwhelm children—as well as adults. Sometimes these feelings can be scary, so children need to be reassured that these hard feelings, such as anger, sadness, or frustration, will fade a little. Happier, brighter ones, such as joy and gladness, will show up once more, allowing them to talk about the positive and loving memories of their pet.

People sometimes stress the importance of a pet to an only child. In some families this may account for some of the strong attachment, but this is not necessarily a bond confined to one-child families. I was not an only child, but my bond with all my childhood animals was strong, and I viewed them as family members, making them cakes and buying them Christmas presents. I was a sickly child, so was often home in bed, absent from school. Perhaps that accounts for a strong bond. I even took my goldfish to university with me, and my fish shared my living quarters in a student residence for three years.

The love many children have for animals is a common phenomenon and one that Western society has used to its advantage concerning books, films, toys, and other marketing paraphernalia. Zoos, petting zoos, and vacations to farms are geared to the childlike attraction to the nonhuman animal. Certain television series tap into the animal attraction. As a child I could never watch a complete episode of *Lassie* without ending up in tears way before the end!

No matter the age of the child, try not to trivialize the death or brush if off because it is too painful to face. You, the parent, will likely be grieving too, but your children may need guidance during this sad time.

Sometimes, either as a way to shield their own pain or out of fear of talking openly about death, adults tell lies to children about pet loss. These range from "Your pet was so good that God decided he needed [insert name] in heaven," to "I'm sorry, but [insert name] ran away," or "[insert name] is living on a farm now." If God needs your pet because of its fine nature, what does that say about people who do good things? Are they going to die because they are good? What does it say about God? Would you want to believe in a God who removes the good from the world because God wants them with him? That is almost enough of a reason to be unkind or unruly. If God is a loving God, allowing your pet to die *because* of its lovely nature runs counter to God's nature.

If you say, "Your pet ran away" or is now "living on a farm," other questions may arise. "What farm? Why?" Watch out as you fumble for more words, forming more lies. If your child believes that your pet ran away, the child may again wonder why. Perhaps it wasn't due to an opened gate, but in a child's mind it might be because she didn't love her pet enough. So now guilt is involved. The child may also fret and always hope that their pet will return home one day. When it rains, or there is a thunderstorm or snow, the child may worry about their lost pet. This causes more—not less—trauma.

If the child finds out that their pet had died and that you lied, there is a strong likelihood that they will not believe you in other matters. Remember, this is a crucial topic and has to be handled correctly, with honesty and integrity—and with tears.

Going and purchasing another pet that "looks the same" also falls into this category of deceit. The fish or rabbit might look similar, but the personality is different, and your child is not stupid. Your child might believe it is the same animal, but as time goes on, they will probably realize that this is not their initial pet.

Sometimes the way something is phrased can convey the wrong message. Statements like "Your pet has gone (or was put) to sleep" can be confusing. "Your pet has gone." Gone where? "Your pet has passed." Huh? "Gone to God" may sound comforting, but partnered with "God needed [insert name]" sets up a picture of a greedy, cruel deity. The child might argue that they needed their pet more than God did. It may not help the formation of healthy religious or spiritual beliefs.

One way to help children acknowledge their grief and find comfort is through stories. If you had a pet when you were a child, you may want to tell stories about growing up with a pet, accompanied by photographs, if you have any. What was special about your animal companion? What did it mean to you to have a pet? Did your dog make you more confident—perhaps walking the dog and meeting other children with pets? Did your pet make you more considerate? Perhaps you were in charge of filling up the water bowl or feeding them each evening. Ask your child to tell you stories about their deceased pet. Remember, everyone in the household may have different recollections and memories; there are no right or wrong answers.

If there are other animal companions, maybe ask your child what their story might be. Did the dog like the recently deceased cat? Based on the answer, what might be the dog's recollections? This may be the time to remind them that the other pets may be feeling sad too and may need extra hugs or attention. Watch that the other pets do not pine too much, to the extent of not eating. Some pets grieve deeply when others die.

Then consider what your child likes to do. Does your child enjoy crafts? Photography? Writing stories? Creating art? Sometimes the act of writing or crafting something in memory of the deceased pet aids healing, and it can be a catalyst to a discussion about death and how they are feeling. Framing a new or favorite photograph of the deceased pet can be a useful activity, as can framing or laminating a drawing your child has done of their animal companion. Journaling is another activity that can combine both the written and the visual, stories and photographs.

If you don't want to start from scratch, there are pet loss journals available for purchase. *Paw Prints in the Stars* is quite special and contains a tear-jerking poem, replete with pearls of wisdom. One of these pearls addresses the pet's possessions. In the poem the pet says they don't mind if their toys, water bowl, or other items are put away, out of sight, if seeing them distresses the grieving owner. These thoughts conclude with this sensitive reminder: "It doesn't mean our love is being put away." The journal includes exquisite illustrations of pets outlined in the night sky (you may wish to sit outside and "see" your pet among the stars), lined pages for stories or photos to be inserted, and a special ribbon for pet tags.

If your pet died near a holiday like Christmas, or if a holiday brings up bittersweet memories of time spent with your pet, crafting a holiday decoration in memory of the deceased pet can be therapeutic. Try drawing a picture of how they "helped" at that time or writing a story concerning these activities, and then share them with other members of the household.

Books to Guide Conversation

Although I wrote about spiritual beliefs in chapter 2, it is worth remembering that, following the death of a pet, it is important to share your views and beliefs about the afterlife with your children, either if they ask you or if you think it might bring them some comfort. Several books address religious beliefs, including the previously mentioned *Samsara Dog*, and the concept of heaven, more specifically, "animal heaven." If you are uncertain about your personal beliefs or about whether animals have souls and participate in the afterlife in some form, try to steer the conversation so that it addresses the issue in a way that is helpful but does not compromise your beliefs or lack of beliefs. It is about being truthful, not telling lies to make either you or your child feel better. Sometimes half-truths are told to deflect strong emotion. If you are unsure about your beliefs, or what happens after death, say that, but maybe couch it in a more general chat concerning life cycles, looking at changes in the seasons and changes in ourselves (from baby to elder).

Books can be an entry point into the topic of pet death. We have been truly blessed by the number of excellent picture books that have been written about pet loss. Sometimes reading a book together can be a time of healing; it may even begin the healing process. Crying over the dog dying in a story can be tears for their own pet, but a little removed, somewhat detached, less threatening. When I was a child, I tried to read *Black Beauty*, but gave up because I kept crying. I understand that it has a very moving section about Beauty's death (see, I still haven't been able to reread it!).

I did, however, discover Paul Gallico's *Thomasina*, which is poignant, and even watched the film based on the book. Yes, I did cry (a lot!), but even as a child, I remember being impressed by the author's knowledge of cats. Later I learned that Gallico was a cat lover and had written a number of books about cats, including the brilliant *Jennie*.

After a family pet has died, I suggest informing not only your child's teacher but also the school librarian, if they have one. The school library, or your local library, may have a collection of picture books dealing with the death of a pet. If a child's pet is aging or critically ill, some of these books may help prepare the child for the pet's eventual demise. I would encourage these books to be part of a whole family activity, because the topic could raise questions, even touch on unfamiliar or scary feelings. I don't mean to suggest that grief will be canceled or dealt with before the sad day! Hopefully certain things will have been anticipated, such as the care of the body, how to remember their pet, and sad feelings.

When we speak about pet loss, it is worth remembering that that term can apply to situations that are not about the death of an animal. Pet loss can mean a pet not being a constant presence in a family, due to divorce. If one parent has custody or has taken on the responsibility for the pet, then the children need to be informed about visiting rights, to allow them to still see their pets, if that is possible. Sometimes geographical factors—such as moving a long distance—preclude this from happening. If this is the case, consider setting up videoconference time with the pet.

When an animal has run away or been stolen, this loss is an enormous grief, because no one knows if the animal companion is still alive and might possibly return one day. This crisis can activate severe anxiety issues, so parents may need advice from the school counselor or from other health professionals. Of course, children are not the only ones in the family affected, so support or counseling might be needed in order to assist other family members.

A recent picture book that deals with this topic is *Olive*, by Edwina Wyatt. The book starts out with a "lost" poster on Lilah's fence, stating that her cat Olive is missing. The book deals very well with emotions associated with grief. Olive does not return. When the family accepts this, they work out ways to navigate through their grief, one being the planting of an olive tree in memory of their cat. Although this ritual seemed a good idea, Lilah doesn't want anything to do with the tree; she just wants her cat Olive. Lilah doesn't water the tree, preferring to neglect or ignore it. Even when it flourishes and provides some shade in the summer, Lilah continues to have nothing to do with the olive tree, because she doesn't want to remember her Olive. Eventually she starts to forget what her cat looked and smelled like. Time goes by. One day a cat wanders in, but Lilah proceeds to chase the cat away. The next day the cat returns and sits on what was Olive's fence. Lilah scares it away, but the cat runs away and climbs up Olive's olive tree. Lilah, continuing to chase the cat, climbs up the tree, but as she does so, she starts to remember, and sees Olive everywhere: "It was Olive's tree. With silvery leaves the color of her paws. Emerald fruit the shade of her eyes."

This book addresses the emotional rollercoaster of grief. The visceral emptiness, the lack of a body to mourn, and no answers concerning your pet's whereabouts, or even if they are dead or alive, make grief messy and troubling. In grief, the air is peppered with "if onlys" and "what ifs."

Several picture books tackle aging, educating about changes that occur as a pet (or human) ages, preparing one for the inevitable. One story, *Missing Jack* by Rebecca Elliott, describes the deceased cat as "like an old furry Grandpa." That the cat would invite the mice in for afternoon tea, rather than chasing them, echoes visiting aging grandparents. Elliott also describes the aging process in a particularly poignant but real way by describing the cat as "fading away." The aging process, for humans and nonhumans, can certainly be described as a "fade," be it memory, physical abilities, or cognitive skills. It may help one prepare for, or at least adjust to, the likelihood of an impending death.

This concept of fading may be brought in to assist in another possible scenario. Sometimes children (and adults) become anxious and upset when the image of their deceased loved one begins to blur or fade, when they can no longer remember them as clearly and as distinctly as before. Being prepared beforehand or by hearing a story like *Missing Jack* may help in knowing that this "fade" is a normal component of grief, and it does not mean that the adult or child does not love the deceased.

Although many of the books deal with aging and associated diseases, one book focuses on death due to an accident, which means that the child has not been prepared for the pet's death, and shock is part of this tragic mix. In *Harry & Hopper*, Hopper is killed in an accident. Harry finds out when he arrives home from school. This book really addresses the individuality of grief and giving people time to grieve in their own way. Harry doesn't want to say goodbye to Hopper, or to be present at his backyard burial. Harry can't concentrate on watching television or his normal activities. His father seems to understand and makes up a bed for Harry on the couch because Harry doesn't want to stay in his bed without Hopper's nightly presence.

That night Harry dreams of Hopper and sees him as he was. They go outside to play. The next night Hopper appears at the window, and the following night, Harry "sees" Hopper again, this time lying by the door, but the image of the dog is starting to fade. Harry brings Hopper indoors, to his bedroom, and onto the bed and is finally able to say goodbye to his friend, in his own time. This book is beautiful because it dares to deal with an uncomfortable topic (death caused by an accident) emphasizing the individuality of grief and the importance of time. It also gives a tick to parents who try to be understanding.

I have not found a book that deals with the death of an animal at a young age due to illness. Such a book would be helpful and is needed because not every animal companion reaches a ripe old age. Most of the books gauge the narrative around the age of the child—from birth or toddler to adolescence, showing the physical changes in the pet.

Sometimes, as in the case of Jane Yolen's *The Day Tiger Rose Said Goodbye*, Tiger Rose's aging process is spoken of from the point of view of the cat, as she proceeds to "farewell" her world. In the classic *Goodbye Mog*, by Judith Kerr, Mog is getting ready to move on, to sleep, so Mog also says goodbye to her earthly home. The cat, Mog, had been the character in eleven previous books, so it would be interesting to know what effect her death had on her readers.

This concept of "goodbye" is included in the titles of other picture books about pet loss, including *Goodbye, Brecken* by David Lupton, *Goodbye, Mr Muffin* by Ulf Nilsson, and *Saying Goodbye to Lulu* by Corinne Demas.

Saying Goodbye to Lulu is a beautiful, wise book that cannot but help children (and adults) grieving their pet. It begins right at old age, talking about the things that Lulu, a dog, can no longer do, such as climb stairs. Lulu can no longer see or hear very well. What I like is that the girl in the story helps Lulu, taking her outside to smell, putting her old toys near her, covering her with her favorite jumper. She tells Lulu that she loves her but yearns to have Lulu as she was in her youth, able to run, play ball, listen to stories. Lulu's health is failing. Her mother shows her a photograph of when Lulu was a pup, saying that how she is now (not able to stand very well, wetting the bed, unable to see, sleeping a lot) is similar to how she was as a newborn puppy. They talk about the life cycle of Lulu. The next day Lulu dies, while the girl is at school. Her mother asks if she wants to say goodbye, but all she can do is cry. This question is asked again at Lulu's burial. The girl is unable to say goodbye. The narrator talks about what the girl misses about Lulu and illustrates the passage of time by drawing the seasons. When spring arrives, the girl can now say goodbye, because the cherry tree that was planted by Lulu's grave, known as Lulu's tree, is flowering. This is sensitively written, with some insightful suggestions for helping children through grief. There is no quick fix through the sadness of grief. Noting the similarities between newborn and old age is a great way to encompass the circle or cycle of life.

Other picture books cover the care of the remains of the deceased. They consider burials and funerals in ways that make sense for many children and help answer some of the tough or tricky questions parents may be asked. The earliest of these picture books is thought to be *The Dead Bird* by Margaret Wise Brown. Written in 1938, this may be the first children's book about animal death. The tale is about a bird in a park, not someone's pet, so technically this is not the first picture book about pet death.

The children find a dead bird in the park and proceed to bury it. Brown narrates what a dead body is like: cold. This bluntness may be helpful, particularly if a child has had no contact with a dead creature. The children then follow what they know about human death; they organize a burial, complete with flowers, singing, a tombstone, and an epitaph. Every day they visit the grave, place fresh flowers on it, and sing, but—and this is the part I am uncomfortable with—they visit "until they forgot." I don't like the sentiment of forgetfulness. I would prefer something along the lines of the children being too busy to visit the bird's grave, or that over time they visited less frequently. I don't think children forget so easily. They may get distracted, or move on to other activities, but forgetting (and yes, the animal is not a pet, but that doesn't mean the children are without feeling) seems a harsh way to conclude the story. However, for the time, this could have been considered a radical picture book.

Another book that deals with animal death rather than pet death is *All the Dear Little Animals*, which illustrates death as a reality of life. A group of bored children start up their own funeral company to bury dead creatures they find (such as bees, mice, a hamster, birds). The children take on various roles: one digs the grave, another writes a poem to be read, and the other child is the professional mourner (cries at the gravesite). They decorate the graves with crosses or with flowers. They find burying the deceased "fun," which is a strange concept. It all ends as quickly as it began, because the next day the children found something else to so. In the book's favor, it demystifies death, and considers several ways animal burials/funerals could be conducted.

Judith Viorst's *The Tenth Good Thing About Barney* is a gentle book of ritual, naming aloud, and giving form to the ways our pets have been gifts to us. Thinking clearly is diminished when grieving, a trait that the book illustrates when the boy is unable to think of, or remember, the tenth wonderful attribute of his deceased cat. With some wise input from his father, the tenth is celebrated. This book also touches on several physical aspects of grief, including a lack of appetite, and an inability to concentrate during routine activities, such as watching television.

Many books speak of backyard burials or funerals. Some of the rituals coincide with the color of the pet's fur or eyes (dictating the flowers that are used). I have not read any that speak of families that live in flats or apartments and have no yards or outdoor space in which to bury their deceased pets, and cremation is not often mentioned.

Although gallows humor has no place within the pages of books about grief, some picture books deal with death by adding a generous, gentle dollop of humor. When humor is used, it is usually via the deceased pet's point of view. In *Cat Heaven* by Cynthia Rylant, the cat is seen sleeping in an angel's lap, lying on God's bed, even sitting on God's head. The accompanying book, *Dog Heaven*, has illustrations of God turning the clouds into dog beds, and watching over the new arrivals when they sleep so that there will be no bad dog dreams. One humorous part depicts obedient dogs: they sit when asked because they all become good in heaven. A nice touch is the reference to dogs that didn't have a home when they were alive. Now they have homes, and backyards, and couches and personalized food bowls, and are loved. The dogs will greet their human companions when it is time for them to die. I find this portrayal of heaven to be of great comfort. This is a book that reassures the grieving and makes one hope that all unfolds as in this story.

Another book that brings in gentle humor is *Love from Alfie McPoonst, The Best Dog Ever.* The book begins with a full-color spread of a garden and a pet's grave, so we know before we read the story what has happened. The book is a short number of love letters, from Izzy's dog Alfie, and later, from Izzy to Alfie. Alfie's letters describe dog heaven. It is fun because Sky Dogs are "nude" (they do not wear leashes or collars). Alfie says that although he misses being alive and living with Izzy, being in Dog Heaven means that he is now back with his dog mother.

Two other books that deal with pet heaven from the point of view of the deceased pet are *Up in Heaven* by Emma Chichester Clark and *Heaven* by Nicholas Allan. Chichester Clark's book is a sensitive portrayal of an aging dog who dies and then finds herself in dog heaven. The dog observes that heaven is full of beautiful gardens and lakes, great weather, and many friends. Like many picture books about pet loss, the deceased pet can see what is going on in their former home and often will take some action. In Chichester Clark's case, this comes via dreams from deceased Daisy to little Arthur, who is missing her greatly. I do have reservations about this concept of the deceased pet being involved in decision-making (not unique to this book; this concept is used in a number of others). A grieving child could read this book and expect to receive dreams from their deceased pet telling them what to do. What if this does not happen? Would they then conclude that their pet did not go to heaven? And if not, then where did they go? Apart from this element, which can be addressed through conversation, this book tackles several difficult facets of grief.

Allan's book *Heaven* is humorous yet insightful. It begins with Dill the dog packing a suitcase, getting ready for the journey to heaven. Dill and Lily discuss what heaven will be like. Dill's version includes bones, lampposts, and things that smell. Dill is collected by dog angels and taken to heaven. Lily is overwhelmed by the things of Dill's that make her miss him so much. Eventually she finds a stray puppy and remembers the things that Dill said about heaven (being a place of meaty bones, lampposts, and smelly things), which help the new puppy settle in. The final page has Dill looking down from heaven, remarking that the dog will think he is already in heaven.

Another interesting book, which is for all age groups (as are many "children's" books), is *The Heaven of Animals* by Nancy Tillman. It is a poem about what heaven is like for animals. One insight that I find helpful is the reference to animals seeming to stare off into the distance or into space. I am sure most of us have observed that with our own animal companions. Tillman wonders if they are in fact seeing heaven. Tillman says that, in heaven, every pet's name is known, they share in the games, the food is sweeter than on earth, and they all get to do the things they love. Another idea that could bring comfort is being told that your love stays with them, and when an angel whispers in their ears, it is their owner's voice that they hear. When it is your turn to enter heaven, they will recognize you because you will be the age you were on earth, when they were alive. Some comforting, reassuring concepts (though perhaps suspect theological ideas) for all ages.

Goldfish Ghost by Lemony Snicket begins after the death of a pet. This is a quirky book, as one might expect from Snicket, but there is a fragility and sweetness about the way he writes about death. The narrative embraces new beginnings. A goldfish has died and floats away from his bowl, trying to find some company, or perhaps the place where he now belongs. As he drifts through his seaside town, we notice in the illustration a boy standing outside the pet shop holding a new goldfish in a plastic bag. Is this his previous owner? If so, Snicket does not stop to ponder the acquisition of a new pet so soon. The goldfish, now a ghostfish, drifts past the beach front, where we notice ghosts wearing old-fashioned swimsuits. Finally he hears a voice coming from the lighthouse. It is the voice of the former lighthouse keeper, who is now a ghost. He swims toward her and is placed in the light, where they are now at peace, keeping each other company. It is a strange yet comforting book, speaking of finding kindred spirits after death, demonstrating that the afterlife need not be feared, and that there is a place for everyone. Was Snicket's placement of the ghostfish in the lighthouse's light a theological nod? Did the ghostfish travel "toward the light"? At the beginning of the story, we learn that the goldfish was born on the surface of the water. Of course, this means that the fish had died, but this is an interesting and thoughtful take on the subject and may be a very helpful book to have on hand for sudden deaths or if pets have very short lives.

An interesting book, which is really about having the grieving child "own" his or her feelings, is *Tough Boris* by Mem Fox. This story deals with the bond between "tough" people and their pets. Boris the pirate was tough, but when his parrot died he showed his emotions by crying. I think this book suits a certain market and helps children, particularly boys (or grown men), know that crying is fine and that tears can be a physical, visible sign of our love, especially when we are grieving. One does not have to bottle emotions or push them down. Perhaps if parents are willing to show their emotions and their vulnerability, this may assist their children to be brave too.

Feelings, and different ways to grieve, are the underlying narrative in *I'll Always Love You* by Hans Wilhelm. The boy is the only one in the family who told Elfie the dog that she was very much loved. Every night before Elfie settled down to sleep, he whispered those words to her. Even though he knew his siblings loved her, even if they never said it, he felt better that he had been telling her that for all their time together. The book concludes with the boy saying that, whenever he gets another pet, he will continue that tradition. Does that mean that his brother and sister were wrong? No, instead it highlights that we are all different.

In *Toby* by Margaret Wild, the girl, Toby's primary carer, ignores him as he becomes old and sick. This seems quite shocking, even callous, until we see that the girl has gone downstairs during the night to give Toby a cuddle before he goes to the vet the following day to be euthanized. This book not only mentions euthanasia as an option, but looks at the different ways of grieving, including anticipatory grief. It helps families recognize that people deal with grief in different ways. Being angry doesn't mean you are not grieving.

Toby is one book which mentions euthanasia. Unfortunately, a number of the picture books about pet loss depict the ill or elderly pet waiting out their time, dying a natural death, which in real life does not necessarily mean a pain-free exit! I find this unhelpful. Yes, some animals die in their sleep, but the majority are brought into a veterinary practice to be released from their pain by being euthanized. In an ideal world, we would all die in our sleep, human and nonhuman, but this is not what happens to the majority of us.

I'll conclude this overview of picture books about pet loss by mentioning a beautiful book, *The Invisible Leash* by Patrice Karst. Zack's dog Jojo has died, and he is grieving. His friend says she understands because her cat died. She said that what helped her was being told that there is an invisible leash that connects the hearts of deceased pets and their owners together, forever. It takes some time for Zack to grasp this, especially after being told that this place is "beyond a place our eyes can see." Zack finds that difficult to believe because he only believes what he can see. His friend continues to explain. By the end of the story, Zack realizes that the most important things are things that cannot be seen but are felt by the heart. He feels a tug, like a leash, in his heart and believes that Jojo is pulling him, from beyond where he can see. Near the end of the book, there is an illustration of pets in heaven, or in the beyond, watching their owners. In the final illustration, the moon shines enough light to allow the reader to "see" some of the billions of "invisible" leashes, connected to their owners. This is a very comforting book, which dares to address the difficult nature of belief and what it means to believe in something we cannot see. It also affirms the power of love and introduces the concept of an afterlife for animals.

It is good to give children access to many books about pet loss because they all deal slightly differently with the subject matter, but I must add a note of caution. There have been a couple of books published that tend to err on the side of gallows humor. I would suggest, if possible, that you have a quick read of the book before sharing it, so there are no unwelcome surprises later. A preread prepares you as well, and may highlight what might be missing or what you may need to raise. Books can be a way in, to speak about loss, about death, about feelings, and about rituals.

Sometimes reading a book together can allow the parent or care-giver to step back from his or her own pain, to be more present with the child. It can allow one to be removed from the rawness of one's own grief. Having said that, I would advise, wherever possible, to talk frankly about the loss. If you are finding it hard to talk, perhaps because your child doesn't want to (adolescents may push down or deny their feelings), then, if appropriate, broach the subject via a short letter or note. This gives the older child or teenager time to digest what you are feeling and thinking and allows them space to voice their own feelings. Give the child the option of writing a note or sending it as a text. Remember, everyone grieves differently.

Comfort, Goodbyes, and Euthanasia

Before we bring the chapter to a close, here are a few thoughts about further ways to hold on to memories, the language of "goodbye," and children's presence at a pet's euthanasia.

When it comes to holding on to memories, sometimes the grieving child or adolescent uses objects associated with their deceased pet to bring them some degree of comfort. These transitional objects might be the pet's blanket or other bedding. It could be the collar. Sometimes the collar is placed in a special place in the house. Perhaps the cat's collar is worn as a bracelet by the child (or by an adult). These items, and others, such as feeding bowls, might be placed in a special drawer or box, becoming objects of ritual, of remembrance, or memory. Even opening the lid and taking a deep breath, smelling the scent of the deceased pet, can be of great comfort. Nothing that helps us travel through grief is odd, or wrong. Even if parents, or siblings, do not understand, that is not the point. The point, or use, of these items is to bring some measure of comfort during grief or to have a permanent reminder of a much-loved deceased family member.

The parent may think more action is needed or the child may voice or suggest what he or she might find helpful. It might be obtaining a new pet (see chapter 5), and several of the picture books I mentioned address this topic. Another option might be for the child (depending on their age) to volunteer at an animal shelter or donate some money to an animal cause, and be kept up-to-date about those particular programs. The child's action may be as simple as buying a can of dog or cat food each week and donating it to a local animal shelter on a regular basis. Giving back can be helpful for both the recipient and the giver.

Many clients ask: How do we say goodbye? Discussing this with a child needs to be done with a note of caution. "Saying goodbye" to Granddad after he has visited does not mean that he will die before his grandchild gets to visit him again. Keep in mind the age and personality of the child and the literal interpretations children can attach to various concepts.

The age of the children and their personalities, combined with the parents' willingness to aid them through the death, come into play when the question is asked, "Should my child attend the euthanasia?" Most veterinarians consult with parents, asking them if their children will be attending. Most veterinarians, or vet nurses, will explain the process of euthanasia to the family. If the child is frightened, I would encourage them to just pat their dog or cat on the head or hold their parent's hand while they do that. They do not have to see the needle.

What they (and their parents) need to be told is that the process is very quick. Sometimes veterinarians forget that this might be the first time that this family (or individual) has had a pet euthanized. Openness and honesty are key ingredients. If the veterinarian uses the words "put to sleep," the parents should be alert to this, being ready to explain what that term means when their children settle to sleep that evening.

Transformative experiences, such as death, can carve deep wounds within young hearts. Sadly, the death of a much-loved pet can be a child's first experience of death, so this event needs to be acknowledged and taken seriously. Listening to their concerns and answering questions with honesty can help provide them with valuable tools. Sitting together through the messiness of it all or voicing the questions of the heart (of the young and not-so-young) will not bring back the deceased loved one, but it may bring to light some memories that aid healing, or it may be an experience that can be looked back on with fondness.

Perhaps the act is a simple, impromptu one, such as sitting outside in the dark together, gazing up at the night sky, or sharing tears while gazing at a photograph. In a society where there seems to be a "quick fix" for most things, one of life's keys is that there is no "quick" or short-cut way through grief, and that no one is left untouched by grief during their lifetime. If one loves, there will be grief. These are hard but crucial life lessons; the hardest and sharpest are often found in the softest of fur.

HEARTBEAT

A small pet is often an excellent companion for the sick or long chronic cases . . .

—Florence Nightingale, 1859

FLORENCE NIGHTINGALE, CREDITED as the founder of modern nursing, was also an author, inventor, and philanthropist. She adored cats. At one time she had seventeen cats, and she is thought to have owned sixty during her lifetime.

Florence also had an unusual pet, in the form of a wild owlet, whom she named Athena.

On June 5, 1850, Nightingale was visiting the Parthenon. During her time there Florence noticed a group of boys tormenting a little owl that had fallen from its nest. Florence, ever the nurse, immediately rescued the little fledgling and kept it. She named this fluffy little owl Athena, after the goddess of wisdom and war. This was symbolic, for a small owl, known as *Athene noctua*, was the sacred bird of Athena. The goddess (and her Roman counterpart, Minerva) was often depicted with a small owl perched on her shoulders or hands.

The trip back to England was taxing for this young owl, whom Florence nurtured and hand fed morsels of meat. The crew fed the owl an incorrect diet and she became ill, but somehow she managed to survive. Athena had tried to work her way out of her cage and was quick to peck at fingers that strayed too close to her. After some time spent in "taming" her, Athena became much calmer, even bowing on command. She took to sleeping in her mistress's lap and being hand fed.

The owl became Florence's constant companion, taking up residence during the day in a large pocket in Nightingale's apron, or in a bag. She would perch on Florence's finger, watching what was going on about her. At the Nightingale residence, Athena would perch on top of a bookcase, suitably in between statuettes of Mercury and Theseus, among the gods, swooping down on unsuspecting flies and occasionally food on the dining table.

Athena became part of Florence's kit. According to her sister, Parthenope, who wrote a book about Athena, on one occasion "she assisted greatly in the cure of a little burnt child, who suffered dreadfully when her wounds were dressed, but in the contemplation of Athena's bows and curtsies opposite her bed (brought for that especial purpose) forgot her woes, and lay quite still while she was doctored daily—the charm continuing undiminished till the cure was complete."

Athena became a popular visitor, welcomed by Florence's elderly, blind great-aunt. Parthenope noted, "She looked upon Athena as a great great niece, and enquired after her visitor's comforts with the same dignified and hospitable care that she shewed for her Mistress. And Athena returned the interest by hopping on her knee or her shoulder as she sat by the fire & settling herself comfortably there for a snooze, while the blind old lady never shewed the smallest fear or surprise at this strange & unaccustomed invasion of the quiet routine of her life."

In 1854, during the cholera epidemic in London, Athena would accompany Florence on house calls, popping her head out of her pocket to gaze upon the patient. In a sense, this little owl became a therapy animal, for the bird was of interest and served as a distraction to many patients.

Florence eventually contracted the disease and was confined to bed. During this time, Athena's loyalty was evident. She stayed close to her mistress, and became a type of "nursemaid." Athena perched nearby, chatted to Florence, and embarked on mini flying sprees around the room. Her manners did need some improving though. Florence's sister wrote, "Every meal she considered to have been brought for her especial use, and she accordingly appropriated the bread and butter, or pounced upon the chicken . . . but her Mistress let it be."

War broke out in the Crimea, and Florence, who had nearly recovered from her illness, was asked to tend to the injured. Florence knew that she could not take Athena with her, that a war zone was not a safe place for a pet, so she left Athena in the care of her sister, and during this time she was placed in the attic. Sadly, it seems that Athena was neglected by the other members of the household. She was so used to being hand fed and had become so domesticated that she probably wouldn't have been able to survive on the odd mouse or rat that made its way into the attic. Athena was also lonely, being apart from her constant companion of five years. Athena perished in the attic when family members failed to check on her.

Florence rushed back after hearing the sad news. She extended her trip by several days and found a taxidermist to preserve her dear owl's body. When Athena's body was returned, Florence held Athena's stiff body and wept. She uttered, "Poor little beastie, it was odd how much I loved you."

In a letter Nightingale wrote to her sister from Turkey, she told Parthenope about encountering an owl on her walk home from the hospital. This brought to mind memories of her dear departed Athena, and Nightingale wrote, "Athena came along the cliff quite to my feet, rose upon her tiptoes, bowed several times, made her long melancholy cry, & fled away—like the shade of Ajax—I assure you my tears followed her."

Nightingale kept Athena in her family home for the rest of her life, and after her death, the owl remained with Parthenope. Athena now resides in the Florence Nightingale Museum in London.

A Middle English poem, "The Owl and the Nightingale," offers a poetic description of a debate between the two birds. Needless to say, it is not as interesting, or as heart-breaking, as the story of the bond between this owl (Athena) and this nightingale (Florence).

4

BURIED HEARTS

Rituals of Remembrance

A DOG LOVER once said, "Someone asked me what the most difficult thing about having a dog was. I replied: the goodbye." Of course, this is true in any relationship. Death is part of life.

I write haiku. This form of poetry lends itself to the way I grieve, when I am diminished, only able to utter short sentences, or am lost for words (a strange state for a preacher!). Overcome by the death of my beautiful Rosa, all I could offer at the time were the seventeen-syllable form of haiku, to match her seventeen years of life:

> *Old haiku dog still.*
> *In earth her seventeen years*
> *toll five, seven, five.*

In the introduction, I shared a myth about how death came into the world via an animal, Coyote. In some cultures, animals have played a role in the permanency of death, as well as in some of the rituals associated with burial and the afterlife. In Zoroastrianism, dogs are seen as clean, righteous animals, possessing special spiritual virtues. One of their spiritual gifts is their special connection with the afterlife. After a human has died, the dog is part of a funerary rite called the "Sagdid." The sacred dog's stare is said to restore purity, lessen infections, and drive away demons from the corpse. Zoroastrians believe the Chinvat Bridge, a sifting bridge, separates the world of the living from the world of the dead. Souls of the just cross over it to enter the world of what lies beyond. This bridge is guarded by two four-eyed dogs.

In some religions, animals have been viewed as bridges between heaven and earth, cast as soul-bearers, accompanying human souls to the afterlife or taking part in judging the deceased. In ancient Egypt, Anubis, the jackal or dog-headed god, was the guardian of the body and soul of the deceased (in earlier times he devoured the dead). Later, Anubis became known as the god who discovered the process of mummification, and thereby became known as the embalmer and the protector of graves. Statues of Anubis were placed in tombs to watch for intruders and grave robbers. Anubis was also involved in judging the dead, working alongside Osiris in the great Hall of Judgement. On one of my bookcases, I have a statue of Anubis bent over an Egyptian sarcophagus, perhaps involved with the mummification process. Sometimes I find myself mulling over this jackal-headed god, liking the idea that, in the past, animals were thought to play a role in our final days. In other cultures, animals acted as escorts, or psychopomps (from the Greek meaning the "guide of souls"), often escorting the human over a bridge to the afterlife.

We buried Merry in the backyard with many tears.
Cannot believe that one little soul can leave such a
large hole in one's life.

—Client

Animal Burial Practices

Does an animal play a role in the ritual of burial? It is interesting to note that in a Jewish midrash, the *Pirke de-Rabbi Eliezer*, a raven showed Adam the practice of burial. The raven had dug a hole and buried its dead companion. When Adam saw this, he did the same and buried Abel.

Rituals provide structure and can help one contain or express emotion. If we think about significant humans in our own lives who have died, we may know what we feel is necessary, what we see as helpful, and what we may vehemently dismiss as macabre, creepy, or even just a bit "over the top" concerning mourning practices. Some of the ways we honor and mourn our animal friends are the same, or similar, but in some cases they can diverge and have a different set of rules or circumstances that one must navigate.

Practices for the burial of my own animal companions have differed, depending on the animal. Our nineteen-year-old cat, Buber, was laid to rest at our previous home, as was another cat in another garden in a previous state and home. Outside our dining room, I know that our dogs Rosa and Primo keep watch near the front gate. Further along is where our Zen cat Pigeon rests, near a water feature, in sight of a statue of Buddha. Not all have their final resting places outside. Sox, an elderly cat, a late addition, is in an urn on my desk. He did not bond with our home after his adoption, so I thought he would prefer to be close to me; hence his container of ashes rests on a shelf on my desk.

Some of us need to physically visit our beloved deceased, animal or human; others prefer to think of them as released, or scattered to the elements, "set free." Being able to leave a flower, or have the physicality of place, is important for many and is even viewed as an essential component to help or ease their grief. (We note how upset people can be when their loved ones are lost at war or die as a result of an accident such as a fire, or cyclone, and the remains cannot be returned to loved ones.)

There is diversity: cultural significance, spiritual diversity, religious needs, and communities inform the way one grieves. Burial or cremation? This is an important decision to make, one that may have already been made due to religious beliefs. In Islam, cremation is deemed as *haram*, an unclean practice. It is believed to be a violation of the body's dignity. In Judaism, customs vary across the movements. For the Orthodox and the Conservative movements, cremation is prohibited, and the body is buried intact. In the Reform tradition, cremation is allowed. In Christianity, cremation is permitted by most denominations, but it is opposed by the Eastern Orthodox Church (which includes the Greek Orthodox Church and the Russian Orthodox Church). In Hinduism and Buddhism, cremation is the preferred method because of reincarnation. Cremation is seen as the quickest way to release the soul and help with reincarnation, the body being just the vessel for holding the soul.

Finding the appropriate way to bid farewell to a much-loved pet is not something new. There is evidence of this practice taking place nearly two thousand years ago. Back in 2011, nearly six hundred animal graves were unearthed in an archaeological dig, but results about them and their purpose were not released until 2021. The majority were cats, but there were also dogs and several other animals, including imported monkeys. The site, which was the early Roman port of Berenice, was on Egyptian land along the coast of the Red Sea. It seems that the graves were in existence between the second and first centuries CE, when Berenice was a busy Roman port. Although old graves containing animals have been found elsewhere (see chapter 1), archaeologists surmise that these animal graves were purely for the use of treasured animal companions or pets. In other words, this could be the earliest record we have of the first pet cemetery. Many of the cats are wearing collars (including one made from bronze), necklaces, or other pieces of adornment. The cats seem to have been placed in individual graves, some covered with pieces of pottery, like a sarcophagus, or with material.

It is interesting to note that some of the animals appear to have been elderly or ill, with injuries, but not injuries sustained through ritual or religious sacrificial practices, and none were mummified. Some of the elderly have few teeth, perhaps due to gum disease. They clearly would have been cared for and fed, as those with injuries and a lack of teeth would not have been able to fend for themselves. All these factors rule out the possibility that these animals were being set apart for sacrifice, were kept in order to keep down the rodent population, or to act as guard dogs. This evidence points to a strong emotional bond between animal owners and their pets.

Some researchers, including Professor Robert Losey, an archaeologist at the University of Alberta, have questioned whether Berenice was the oldest pet cemetery, citing examples in Europe and Russia, where hunter-gatherer groups buried their dogs, sometimes with grave goods, nearly seven thousand years ago. A famous site is in Russia's Lake Baikal region. The most famous of the dog burials took place on a slender piece of land that extends out into the water at the south end of the lake. This site, known as Shamanka 11, contains the remains of about 150 humans. This was a special place reserved for burial, not for residing. The site contains the grave of a dog, buried with a carved antler spoon, which would have been a valuable object. It appears that this dog was laid to rest according to the same funerary traditions as those of the humans and was valued. Losey affirms this claim, adding, "To them it was a member of the family. It had a soul."

Many of us know that the Victorians loved their pets, and companion animals took on a whole new mode of being, including some cemeteries allowing Victorians to be buried with their pets. This practice fell out of favor, but since the 1990s has seen a comeback in Britain, with this practice crossing the Atlantic. In 2015, New York passed a law allowing animal companions to be buried with their owners.

The first pet cemetery in the UK was established during Victorian times and gives an insight into the devotion of many Victorians to the fairly new concept of pet ownership. This pet cemetery was, however, unplanned, an accident really. It was established in Hyde Park, in 1881, with the inaugural burial of Cherry. This little Maltese terrier used to go through Hyde Park every day on her daily walk. After she died of old age, Cherry's family asked Hyde Park's gatekeeper whether Cherry could be buried in the private back garden of the gatekeeper's home, Victoria Lodge. It was a spot the dog loved. The gatekeeper, Mr. Winbridge, knew the family and agreed. Cherry's tiny tombstone reads: "Poor Cherry. Died April 28 1881." The next pet to be buried there was Prince, a Yorkshire terrier, whose owner was the Duke of Cambridge. Poor Prince had died due to a fatal accident. After Prince was buried there, word got out and Hyde Park pet cemetery became the place for the deceased pets of the wealthy to be laid to rest. Mr. Winbridge usually carried out the burial, but owners were often too overcome by grief to attend. In 1892 one bereft owner, Lord Petre, sent his deceased pet to be buried, promising that he would attend the burial the following morning. Sadly, during the night Lord Petrie died. Some wondered if he had died of a broken heart. Over the years, until its official closure in 1903, over one thousand pets, mainly dogs and cats, but also birds and other creatures, were buried there. The occasional burial was still carried out, however, until 1976. Some of these graves had small headstones, often with phrases which were similar to those found on human graves of the time: "Rest in peace" and "We are only sleeping." Several had Bible passages inscribed on their headstones, which raises the question concerning whether this meant the pet owner believed that animals, or, in this case, specifically pets, had souls.

Another famous British pet cemetery is located in Ilford, Essex. The Ilford Animal Cemetery was set up in the 1920s by the People's Dispensary for Sick Animals (PDSA) charity and has approximately three thousand burials in its grounds. The cemetery was closed to burials in the 1960s, but pet tags are still placed on memorial pillars. This cemetery is also the final resting place of famous military animals which received the Dickin Medal (the animal equivalent of the Victoria Cross). Buried here are thirty-two pigeons, eighteen dogs, three horses, and one cat. The cemetery fell into rack and ruin, very much neglected, but thanks to funding it was restored in 2007.

Among the graves of pets and military animals, there is a marker highlighting the less fortunate: "The Strays and All Ill-Treated Animals." During the first week of World War II, over 750,000 dogs, cats, and other pets were euthanized in Britain, due to mass hysteria. Owners were worried about food shortages, bombings, and other dangers that might befall their animal companions. The PDSA provided a meadow in its grounds to allow thousands of these pets to be buried.

In the United States, many are familiar with the name Hartsdale, America's first (but now not the only) pet cemetery. Established in 1896 in Dr. Johnson's apple orchard, its oldest remaining headstone, dating from 1899, is for Dotty. Similar to the situation in Hyde Park, this pet cemetery came about in response to a bereaved client's dilemma. Dr. Johnson was a veterinarian and a pioneer in the growing field of animal welfare. At the time, in response to public health laws, the city of New York banned the burial of animals within its limits. The upset client approached Dr. Johnson at his office in Manhattan. Her dog had just died, and she didn't want the body to be disposed of as per the regulations (for pets were not permitted to be buried in public parks or in human cemeteries either). Dr. Johnson offered to bury her dog on his property in Westchester, which he did. It would have possibly remained a one-off burial, except Johnson lunched with a reporter friend and told him about this. To Johnson's surprise, this story appeared in print in the *New York Times*, as did requests from other grieving pet owners wanting a place to bury their loved ones with dignity. Johnson was a compassionate man, a great animal lover, and he set aside three acres of his orchard for pet burial. The many requests Johnson received prompted him to set up a system to make it all flow smoothly. The pets were brought to his Manhattan clinic, and documentation was then carried out. Each pet was in a casket and delivered to the cemetery by train, with their owners arriving separately to attend the burial. The cost of a plot was not cheap: twenty-five dollars for a dog, and twelve dollars for a cat or for another small animal. But if people could afford it, then they were willing to pay for peace of mind and for a place to visit their loved one. At the time, it was expected that the bereaved owners would tend to the upkeep of the plots and supply the monuments and headstones. Today there are over 80,000 animal companions buried at Hartsdale, and approximately 30,000 cremations are undertaken every year.

Some of the words on the monuments and headstones speak loudly to our grieving hearts:

> *He came into my life*
> *for want of a meal and a place to stay . . .*
> *He left with my heart.*

> *The only sorrow you ever brought me*
> *was the day you left.*

In northwest Alabama, a unique and specific dog cemetery has been set aside solely for coonhounds (one has to prove that the dog you plan to bury there is a coonhound). The Key Underwood Coon Dog Memorial Graveyard, where 185 coonhounds have been buried, was set up in 1937 when Key Underwood buried his much loved coonhound, Troop, his friend for over fifteen years, on the site of a popular gathering spot for hunters, an area that Troop knew and loved. It has become well known, and indeed says something about the depths of emotions some hunters feel for their dogs. Although Key Underwood did not set this place up as a cemetery—he had just wanted to bury his dog and mark the spot—he saw a need and allowed it to expand. The headstones vary, made out of wood, stone, or sheet metal, and the epitaphs differ too, but they all bear witness to our bond with our pets.

There is a similar pet cemetery in Australia, established in a remote area, as a testament to much-loved dogs. In Western Australia, near the town of Corrign, situated on the wheatbelt, a local dog, Strike, was buried in 1974. Other dogs have been buried there, headstones added and, in 1992, a large statue of a dog was set up at the entrance of what had now become a dog cemetery, with over two hundred graves. It was a personal witness to the Australian farmers' love of their stock dogs, working dogs that would ride on the back of their utility trucks and help round up livestock. It did not set out to be a tourist attraction (it was never even intended to be a dog cemetery—it had been an approved area for a lone dog burial), but it has ended up as that. More importantly, it has become a testament to the bond between farmers and their dogs. Traditionally, farmers have been portrayed as stoic, speaking little about their feelings. This silence, or reluctance to talk about their emotions, extends to the grief they may experience after a working dog, or pet, has died. This cemetery allows emotions to be expressed in words and in the form of statues erected on some of the graves.

Of course, pet cemeteries have been established in other parts of the world; animal lovers are not limited by nationality, country, or borders. In Paris, the Cimetière des Chiens et Autres Animaux Domestiques ("cemetery of dogs and other domestic animals") was established in a northwestern suburb of Paris in 1899, in similar circumstances to Hartsdale. Hygiene and the spread of germs was an issue, with a law being brought in that prohibited animals being buried near humans. This cemetery sports some wonderful works of art, particularly art nouveau, as well as housing a number of famous animals in its earth, including Rin Tin Tin.

In Japan, because of small dwellings and limited space, having a pet is a privilege. Those fortunate enough to have a pet tend to treat them as if they were a child (if Buddhist, they would know that in Buddhism it is believed that animals have souls). When a pet dies, the majority of pet owners choose cremation (due to constraints of space) over burial. Cremation can take place at a temple, a cemetery facility, or at home. Home cremation is carried out by a mobile cremation company. Representatives of the company meet the owners at home, or in a quiet secluded area. While it may seem strange to westerners to witness cremation of loved ones, this is common practice in many parts of Asia.

In Japan, there are a number of Buddhist temples where much-loved pets can be cremated and their ashes either returned to the human owner or laid to rest on site. If the pet is to be cremated at the temple, the family may gather as prayers are said (by them and by a monk), and incense is lit. The second oldest Buddhist temple in Tokyo is Jindaiji Temple, situated in Chofu Prefecture, in the western part of the city. It houses a pet cemetery in the temple precincts. The pet cemetery opened over sixty years ago and certainly fulfills a need. Outside, there are large gravestones and monuments, as well as outside vaults where a pet's ashes can be interred. Jindaiji Temple also has indoor vaults, and along a number of corridors, shelves house many urns, votive plaques, and objects from the families that were important to their pets. It has become a place families visit to remember their pets and to offer prayers and food. Inside Jindaiji Temple is Banrei To, the "Tower of Souls," a ninety-eight-foot-tall tower. At its base there is a statue of a Buddhist saint, said to be keeping watch over the animals. For many Japanese pet owners, having their pets rest there is a way to honor them. More than 20,000 animal companions have been laid to rest at the Jindaiji Temple, many accompanied by their own funeral rites, with four hundred to five hundred being interred every month.

Unlike in Western countries, euthanasia is rarely performed in Japan. In the majority of cases, the pet is cared for at home, pain being managed by palliative medication and care. According to veterinarian Dr. Chikao Muratani, the topic of euthanasia is not raised: "If I were to ask, I'd be considered a monster and would lose my patients. This is because Japanese people want their pets treated exactly like humans, so they expect doctors to prolong their lives as much as possible." The owners are expected to be with their pets until the end of their earthly lives.

Why have I devoted these pages to what could appear to be nothing more than an interesting history lesson about pet cemeteries? I have done so to emphasize that caring for the remains of our deceased pets, wanting to have a place to visit, or to say farewell to them, is not a new concept, or even confined to Western society. The animal–human bond is intense. It cuts across races, creeds, and countries. The grief that erupts when a beloved animal dies is, as I have stressed before, normal.

Saying Goodbye

What does it mean to feel that we have had a chance to say goodbye? How important is it to personalize the burial or cremation? We have read some examples in picture books in chapter 3 and the stories of Edward Lear and his cat, Foss, and Florence Nightingale and her pet owl, Athena, in the Heartbeats. But what about ourselves? What ways do we bid farewell to our beloved pets? What helps us?

> *Ebony's cremation went very well. She had eight yellow roses and one red rose, rosary beads, her lead . . . and she was wrapped in her favorite pink blanket with prayer cards. My heart is still very broken.*
>
> —Client

Saying goodbye to your beloved animal companion is best when done in a way that offers a fitting tribute to them and aids your own healing. There are many ways to say goodbye: a burial (in the garden or in a pet cemetery), cremation (scattered ashes, or kept ashes, or the setting aside of some of the ashes), or posting a tribute online or via social media. One of my clients commented on the burial bag their pet was placed in after his euthanasia. When I began my work at the animal hospital, deceased animals were wrapped in towels. One vet had pillowcases at the ready. I thought we could do better than either of those and found some beautiful burial bags for pets online. The clients appreciated the beauty of the bag, but also the safety and comfort of it.

Sometimes clients would bring in their own items for burial, often their pet's favorite blanket or bedding, in order to wrap them in it before taking them home. I encouraged the owners to take part in the covering up, if they were up to it. I would also include flowers or rose petals that could be included in the ritual. Toys, such as a dog's much-chewed tennis ball, were placed carefully near or around the deceased pet. This ritual contains echoes of Egyptian burial: items to be used in the afterlife, objects to promote the deceased one's happiness in the next life.

Some people prefer to hold on to objects for the comfort of those left behind. One client wrote about how her other animals were missing the one who had died: "Groucho was a very loved family member and missed by 'the gang' as much as me. . . . Sammi [dog] . . . has given up his good-sized bed and sleeps in Groucho's little one. He can hardly fit in and some of him hangs over the side—his head and a leg or two." She also told me their plans for Groucho's cremation, which included combining them with her husband's ashes: "Groucho has now been cremated and his and [husband's] ashes will be distributed from a balloon by grandchildren as [husband] had requested three weeks before his death."

Burial or Cremation?

Deciding whether to bury or cremate is an important decision that you may have already made, based on religious and personal preferences, physical surroundings and practical issues, and the opinions of your family. If you live in a family unit or in a shared household, a conversation needs to take place. Talking about caring respectfully for your deceased pet's physical body may not be the easiest of conversations, but it is a necessary one.

If you are going to bury your deceased animal companion, you might need to contact your local council before proceeding, because not every municipality allows burial of pets on residential land or private property. If you are renting, or thinking of moving soon or during the next few years, these factors need to be taken into consideration: What will happen to that grave? Will you be able to cope with leaving your loved one behind? Cremation is not always a person's first choice, but it may end up as the only option. If cremation is chosen as a compromise, especially if you had wanted a burial, then consider interment of the ashes in a large potted plant that can be moved with you if you leave that house. Small pets, such as mice, rats, and birds, can be buried in a large potted plant.

> *We miss her dreadfully but know the time had come*
> *for her to leave us and lie in peace in that resting place*
> *in the sky. We feel her very near as her ashes adorn our*
> *bookcase.*
>
> —Client

What to do with the ashes? If you are unsure, keep them, perhaps out of sight, until you have made a decision. Some pet owners know that they will scatter some ashes in their dog's favorite park or walking area (again, you may need to get approval). Others scatter them at home, in the yard, or place them in a potted plant, and others keep them inside. I know of one family who keep them on a shelf near their sofa, in the room where they gather to watch television. They told me that their pet had always liked watching sports with them and that he could continue to do so.

There is really no right or wrong (apart from zoning/council regulations and religious beliefs). It is about what helps you. It may be that you wait until you have a new addition; then you may decide it is time to scatter or bury the ashes in your yard, perhaps asking your deceased pet to watch over your new arrival. If you live with family, ask their advice too.

There are many online groups that help pet owners who are grieving their loved ones. Your veterinarian may know of a local one or may suggest one that operates within your region. There are also sources about bereavement on most pet cremation/pet cemetery websites.

Some may offer suggestions concerning rituals on burial or a prayer for your pet before and after cremation. In chapter 2, I wrote about the dilemma for Jewish pet owners, being advised by some movements in Judaism that they were forbidden to use traditional mourning prayers. There are alternatives, which can be found on a number of websites.

A Simple Service

You may have decided to respectfully care for your pet's remains, either as a body (therefore burial) or as ashes (scattered or interred/buried) at home. You do not need the physical body to hold a service. If you are not burying the body or scattering the ashes, you can still have a memorial or thanksgiving time in memory of your deceased pet, perhaps over a special afternoon tea, with photographs and other tangible items or memories on display. Here are some ideas for a service to honor the memory of your animal companion.

Preparation

If a burial, then the deceased pet will have been placed in a box, pillow-case, rug, towel, burial bag, or other covering. If the deceased pet has been cremated, have the ashes there for scattering or interment. You may want to include the following items in your service.

- Flowers, petals, or leaves.
- A grave marker, such as a piece of sculpture, or a carved stone, or cross, on the site.
- A plant on the grave. If it is the wrong season for planting, or if you want more time to choose an appropriate plant, shrub, or tree, you may wish to make the act of choosing a special time for family members.

If there are items to go into the grave (such as letters, drawings, photos, favorite toys, etc.), have those ready to go. If you are going to have refreshments afterward near the burial plot, have something to sit on. If you are planning on having a toast, have glasses ready, with appropriate beverages ready. If music is to be played, have it set up.

Work out how you want the ritual to unfold. You may want to start with the body in the ground—but not covered by dirt, to allow photos, drawings, or toys to be placed during the service. If that would be too difficult to undertake (for example, with small children), then have everything set in place before beginning. Even if everything is in place, flowers or petals can still be scattered onto the grave during the service.

Reflection

Here are a few guidelines and prompts that might help you shape the service.

> We loved [*insert name*] because . . . [*allow individuals to say what they loved/remember most about their pet*].
>
> What I will miss most will be . . .
>
> Do you remember when . . .?
>
> [*Insert name*] made me a better person because she/he taught me patience/love/loyalty . . .
>
> I loved that she/he kept my secrets . . .

Readings

You may wish to read "The Rainbow Bridge," a verse from Scripture, a meaningful quotation, or a poem. Here are a few ideas:

> *For the fate of humans and the fate of animals is the same; as one dies, so dies the other. They all have the same breath, and humans have no advantage over the animals. . . . All go to one place; all are from the dust, and all turn to dust again. (Ecclesiastes 3:19–21)*

> *In his hand is the life of every living thing . . . (Job 12:10)*

> *You save humans and animals alike, O Lord. (Psalm 36:6)*

Until one has loved an animal, a part of one's soul remains unawakened. (Anatole France)

Some angels choose fur instead of wings. (Unknown)

Someone asked me what the most difficult thing about having a dog was. I replied, "The Goodbye." (Unknown)

Everyone is taught that angels have wings, but the lucky ones of us find they have four paws. (Unknown)

Having a dog will bless you with the happiest days of your life, and one of the worst days. (Unknown)

Prayer of Memories

Here is a prayer of memories that can be done with one or more readers.

Reader: The life spans of our pets are fewer than for humans, and that knowledge brings with it much sadness:

- fewer years to pack in all the activities we want to share with them;
- fewer years for walks, for cuddles, for sleeping with them curled safe in our arms;
- fewer years to tell them secrets, knowing they will never "tell."

We want them to live long lives, with us.

Reader: And yet, we give thanks to our Creator—and their Creator—what a wonderful idea that was to create pets! To have humans share their lives with other species in a very personal and profound way.

- For all the precious memories of [*insert name*], we thank you.
- For the gifts [*insert name*] has left us, including [*name gifts*], we thank you.
- For being a member of our family and living faithfully with [*insert name*], we thank you.

(Note: Now cover or fill the grave. If that action might upset certain individuals, particularly children, cover the site with a towel, and come back later to pack down the soil. Leave something decorative on top such as flowers or a grave marker. If scattering, check the way the wind is blowing. Try a little at a time.)

Reader: We have now laid our much-loved [*insert name*] to rest.

[If burial]: May the earth's protective covering remind [*insert name*] of our love. We covered you with kisses, with hugs, and with more than enough love for your life span and for ours. Be at peace within this earth, within our hearts.

[If scattering]: We now release you, you are free. Our kisses, our hugs, our love, will travel with you into the wind. You are now spirit, free from pain and suffering. Travel safely to our Creator with love, kisses, and hugs.

All: Thank you for living with us, for bringing us much joy and laughter. We will never forget you.

(Note: Depending on your beliefs, you may wish to add: "Until we meet again" or "We believe that our loving God, who created every living thing, will care for you after death, and that we will be reunited when it is our time to make that final journey" or "May God continue to look after us in our sadness.")

Words of Love

If you are going to have a toast, then this is the time to fill glasses and raise them with these words, or something similar.

Reader: To [*insert name*]

All: To [*insert name*]

Reader: We will miss you, but you remain forever in our hearts.

Blessing

Reader: And now we bless our loved one, and hand [*insert name*] over to God. As Helen Keller said, "What we once enjoyed and deeply loved we can never lose, for all that we love deeply becomes part of us."

All: Amen.

Transitional Objects, Keepsakes, and Cards

Apart from attending respectfully to their bodily remains via burial or cremation, what are other ways pet loss is acknowledged?

When my elderly cat died, I received a number of pet loss condolence cards. I have sent many myself, in my professional role and in my personal life. I find them to be of great comfort. They are not only a visible reminder that people are thinking of you as you grieve, but they are also validations that animal loss is normal and that we grieve because we love.

Having said this, I must admit that some cards seem to be more understanding and compassionate regarding the nature of pet loss than others. It must be said that if you are purchasing a pet loss card in a store, the range will be limited; indeed, there may be little or no choice.

There are more choices available online, and some are handmade and personalized. You may even choose to craft your own card to send. The important thing to remember is that by sending a card, you may be letting that grieving person know that this is normal. Pet loss, pet grief, hurts, and there are people who care and understand. Some veterinary practices send out their own personal cards, which I think is a wonderful idea. I am of the strong opinion that the way a veterinary practice deals with grief can make or break its business. People remember who comforted them when their pet died. A card popped in the mail speaks volumes.

Like Groucho's family, many pet owners hold onto keepsakes or mementos: collars, toys, leads, feeding bowls, rugs. In 1951 Donald Winnicott, whose research was based on separation of children from their primary carer, named objects, such as a particular toy or blanket, that brought the child comfort and a sense of security "transitional" items. Grief counselors use that term and also refer to them as "linked objects."

Transitional objects form and keep a connection with the deceased pet, as well as provide comfort to the grieving. This tangible, physical link can have a number of benefits, aside from comforting the grieving. Transitional objects can lower blood pressure and can facilitate the release of the hormone oxytocin, which reduces anxiety and stress. These objects can lower cortisol levels, cortisol being a stress hormone associated with a number of systems, including the immune system and the digestive system.

These objects are physical reminders of the one who has died and a connection to the one grieving. These objects can be the closest alternative to the deceased's physical presence, and, in the case of collars, leads, and rugs, the deceased pet's smell (and possibly markings) may still be present on the object. Sometimes we worry that we may forget our deceased; having transitional objects can help. Looking at the lead, we remember daily walks. The tinkling of the bell on a cat's collar brings to mind our feline's magnificent leaps, and the feeding bowl that of the daily meal regime.

Of course, these objects can produce copious amounts of tears! They remind us of significant and loving relationships, which have now changed. When we grieve, some days (or parts of days) are better than others. Having a transitional object nearby can help, for they may elicit an emotional response. How does this object make you feel? Do you feel better after holding or looking at it? Do you feel stronger?

There is a problem with the term *transitional*, for this implies that this is not an object that will remain permanent. We must exercise some caution. What may have begun as a temporary way to help navigate one's way through grief and later would be set aside or disposed of may, in fact, become a permanent object for the grieving—and that is fine! Some people wear the items: collars become bracelets, a rug may be crafted into a quilt, a portion of a blanket sewn onto a garment as a "memory patch." Leads can become objects of art, hanging from a door handle as a quirky item; food bowls can store a toy or ball. There is no right or wrong.

Having said that, I would add that one should not make decisions based on other people's advice. Some find belongings of the deceased (animal and human) a little creepy, and would advise the mourner to get rid of them. If you are not ready, then do not do so. Otherwise it may become an issue to regret and could become a source of tension within the household. If the other people in the house do not understand your need for these transitional objects, perhaps keep them in your space or a cupboard.

Sometimes someone's reluctance to acknowledge the importance of these items to you is because of their own emotions. If they tell you it is time to get rid of these things, that it is time to "move on," it may be as simple as the fact that they don't want to see you in pain. Try to explain to them that this object brings you comfort. Holding on to a transitional object, such as a collar or lead, may make one feel "wrapped" in their deceased.

One idea, which may appeal to some but not to others, has been to purchase a toy that resembles your deceased pet. Psychologist Tsholofelo Jood said: "Keeping plush replicas of deceased pets helps the bereaved feel connected with their beloved companions, giving them a much-needed element of comfort when they feel lonely and isolated."

This may not be everyone's idea of a suitable transitional object, but it may help some, particularly children.

The Things We Keep

We have touched on transitional objects, so it seems appropriate to mention the keeping or storing of objects on a more permanent basis, those that are in the "to keep" pile. These may include water or food bowls, bedding, toys, leads, collars, and tags. Some of these may be kept to pass on to someone else or kept for your new addition (such as the food bowls or bedding). Others are for sentimental reasons, or as a means of having something your deceased pet used close by. Bedding and collars may still have the scent of your deceased pet on them, so may be an item for hugging or clutching tight. Tags and collars can be made into jewelry or into ornaments or decorations. If you are getting rid of some of these items, taking a photograph of the items before-hand can be therapeutic. I cannot stress this enough: if you are unsure whether or not to keep a certain item, keep it! Store it in a cupboard, or box, until you feel able to make a decision. (And sometimes the decision is to not make a decision. And that is fine!)

If an item doesn't appeal to you, or you do not have a deep emotional attachment to it, check with the other members of your household or family. It may surprise you what appeals to whom—and sometimes even "why." Talking about these items can initiate other stories and memories, so these may assist healing.

Over the years, I have kept several of the food bowls, plus the bedding, in case I use them for the next dog or cat. I never have, but that has been my rationale for keeping them. Collars, leads, and tags are somewhat easier to justify keeping, as are some toys. Again, it is about the emotional connection. The lead is a visible reminder of your spiritual and emotional connection; the round collar is in the shape of a circle, an unbroken bond of love; and the ID tag a visible stamp of their name, which is also invisible, engraved on your heart.

Memorial Jewelry

A category of jewelry that became popular during Victorian times after the death of Queen Victoria's husband Prince Albert was memorial jewelery. These tokens of remembrance for the deceased, in the form of a brooch, ring, bracelet, or necklace, were woven or braided from the hair of the deceased and became a public statement: this person is mourning. But they were also private items of comfort.

This form of jewelry has found favor with a number of pet owners following the death of their beloved animal companions.

Many pet owners keep a lock of fur or several whiskers from their pets, perhaps transferring them into a locket. By this action, it becomes a piece of memorial jewelry. Others prefer to keep these precious items in a special box. Some purchase lockets, or small vials, in which to keep a small portion of their pet's ashes. Pet cremation facilities sometimes have these available on site, so if you are interested in this, do ask at the time that you organize the cremation. If the pet crematorium doesn't offer that service, they may be able to recommend a company or business that does.

Items of memorial jewelry containing the hair, fur, or ashes of much-loved deceased pets tend to be private and intimate items, often only known to their wearer. Why this need for privacy? I think there are two reasons: the first being that, in the West, our culture prefers to ignore or minimize death and grieving. With the exception of some countries and cultures, we no longer feel compelled to dress in mourning clothes—even at funerals. We do not rush out to purchase memorial jewelry, perhaps feeling that it would be a little creepy. However, this type of jewelry has found a market regarding deceased pets. In most cases, the wearing of a locket or vial that contains ashes or hair is not intended to announce to the public that you are mourning. There are times when it is difficult to gauge whether one can tell someone else that one's pet has died, and expect to receive words of condolences or sympathy. Will others understand the magnitude of their loss? The wearing of pet memorial jewelry can bring comfort or peace to the bereft owner.

These items of memorial may be imbued with much importance or reverence, particularly if someone has been unable to bury their loved one's remains.

HEARTBEAT

HACHIKŌ (ORIGINALLY NAMED Hachi) was a white Japanese Akita dog who became famous for his loyalty. His name means "eight"; a name he was given either because he was the eighth pup in his litter or because eight is a lucky number in Japanese culture. Hatchi plus *kō* may mean "prince" or be a mark of respect, like sir.

Hachikō became a familiar sight at the Shibuya train station in Tokyo, but he did not begin his life in a large city. Hachikō was born in Odate City, in northern Japan, in November 1923. After a few months, Hachikō was sent to Professor Hidesaburo Ueno, who lived in Tokyo. Akitas originated in the northern mountains of Japan. They are a fearless breed, having been used by samurai for protection and as guards for royalty. In the past, Akitas hunted wild boar and bears. They would not back down. They are dogs with large, brave hearts.

Akitas become totally devoted to their owners, and this was certainly the case with Hachikō. Though still a pup, Hachikō would make his way to the Shibuya train station in the early evening, waiting for his master to return from the University of Tokyo, where he worked as an agricultural scientist. This daily routine happened every evening.

Then on May 21, 1925, Professor Ueno did not come home. Sadly, he had suffered a cerebral hemorrhage at work and died.

This did not deter the faithful dog. Hachikō continued to go to the train station to await Ueno's return. He had been given to new owners, but he ran away, settling in at the home of Ueno's former gardener (where he stayed during the day) and at the train station.

In the early days at the train station, Hachikō was often shooed away or teased, but in 1932, after an article had been written about this loyal, faithful dog, he became a celebrity. This is when he became known as Hachikō rather than Hachi, the added *kō* being a mark of respect. Regular commuters had been feeding Hachikō, but now he was greeted by many visitors and tourists. Hachikō became a national treasure, a symbol of loyalty, an example for Japanese citizens to imitate. A bronze statue was commissioned, and in 1934 it was placed in the spot where he waited, the dog in attendance at its unveiling. Hachikō continued to keep vigil for his master until he died on March 7, 1935, nearly ten years later. His body was found near the station.

The statue of Hachikō was melted down during the war, for badly needed metal. In 1947 a new statue was made to fill the void, crafted by the son of the original sculptor. The area is also marked with a number of bronze paw prints, a photo of Hachikō, and a sign that reads: "Loyal dog Hachikō."

Every year, on April 8, a service is held to honor Hachikō. The ceremony takes place at the Shibuya train station, and a Shinto priest conducts the ritual, with dignitaries in attendance. By the end of the service, the bronze statue is draped with many floral wreaths.

Hachikō's taxidermied body's fur stands on permanent guard at the National Museum of Nature and Science in Tokyo and is much visited. His story has been told in several films and books, so it is well known throughout the world.

What is quite touching is that there are a number of statues of Hachikō in different places. On the campus of the University of Tokyo, there is a beautiful one of Hachikō and Professor Ueno greeting each other.

What of Hachikō? His skin and fur were preserved, but his ashes were interred next to Professor Ueno's tomb in Aoyama Cemetery.

There is also a monument there. The shrine is visited and food and dog toys left for Hachikō's spirit. I like to think of Hachikō and Ueno together, reunited for eternity.

I marvel that Hachikō was still so young when he displayed such loyalty and devotion, but bonds can be formed in a short time. Perhaps it is something to do with the Akita breed. Sometimes Japanese parents are given a small state of an Akita on the birth of a child, the dog a symbol of loyalty but also of protection, health, and happiness. Maybe though, it has more to do with love than breeding, connection rather than pedigree. Love and heart.

5

HEALING HEARTS

Grief and Gratitude

SO FAR WE have talked mostly about how humans grieve animals' deaths, but we know animals grieve too. You may have witnessed that behavior with one of your animal companions, either after the death of one of your pets or one of the human members of the household.

During the writing of this book, my husband, David, died. Harry, our dog, was besotted with David. After my husband's death, Harry lost his appetite for several days and was very sad and despondent. His tail drooped, and he would sit beside me, keeping me company while I cried.

Harry's mood has improved since David's death, yet he still goes and sits in David's study, by his chair, waiting for him. Whenever David's mobile phone rings, Harry rushes to see who answers it.

What we say about humans' grief can perhaps be said about animals' grief as well. Helen Keller wrote, "What we once enjoyed and deeply loved we can never lose, for all that we love deeply becomes a part of us." Indeed, because of this, grief—for both humans and animals—is not linear, like a calendar. It does not follow a set path or have an end or finish date. Instead, grief is more clock-like, ongoing, and like a heart, it beats, or ticks, with occasional changes in its rhythm and timing.

Grief doesn't end with the burial or cremation, does it? It would be better if it did, but it doesn't. However, you may have had people around you treat the loss as if this were the case. As if you "should be over it by now." There is no quick fix.

Broken hearts hurt, broken hearts don't function well, broken hearts take time to mend, and broken hearts take what seems like an eternity to heal. When they do mend and heal, they are not as they were before. That heart will never be as it was.

You may feel you will never be able to move out of the glue of grief, and, in a sense, you are correct. Grief will always be part of the fabric of your life and of your relationship with your deceased animal companion.

Grief is intensified somewhat by the mere fact that your pet (for most people) lived in your home, in your space. There are reminders everywhere: the emotional, the physical, the memories, the fur. I don't know how it happened, but after my pets died, I would find their fur in so many places, even after I had vacuumed several times. That tuft of cat fur would reduce me to tears.

Back in chapter 1, I spoke about the home, the environment, and how it triggers emotions. Those four walls are held together by memories—the toughest and strongest glue there is! In this chapter, I share some ideas that may help you to heal. This doesn't mean the grief goes away—it won't—but some strategies may help you function better and allow your heart to have a short rest from the exhausting work of grief.

Caring for the Grieving

It is important to repeat: grief is *not* an illness. It is a response—
physical, emotional, and spiritual—to the loss or absence of a loved
one, usually due to their death (although it can also be because of
serious illness, the loved one moving elsewhere, etc.). Having said
that, it is important that we recognize that people (and animals)
grieve differently, and many need assistance during this sad and
overwhelming time. Most societies do not speak of death very well,
speaking about it in furtive whispers, brushing the topic under the
carpet, or disguising it by pushing products that will keep one looking
young (and thereby "cheating" death).

How do you keep going when you find it too hard, or if you can't
find a reason to go on? Sometimes you have a family to care for. That
may be enough to keep you focused on carrying out the day-to-day
things, such as cooking, going to work, and being there as a family at
the end of the day.

Cooking and Eating

During grief, a common ailment is lack of appetite. Food has lost its
appeal, even your favorite dishes may have lost their taste. Grief has an
impact on your physical body, as well as on your emotional and spiritual state. If you find that your food tastes like sawdust or you really
don't feel like eating, try the things weight loss programs caution you
not to do, such as eating in front of the television or computer.

When you eat while doing something else, often you are not
conscious that you are eating (which is why it can lead to weight gain).
In this case, try eating small, easy-to-digest meals in front of a screen to
see if you are able to eat. I am not suggesting you will enjoy your food

yet—eating is associated with emotions, with joy, with family, and with celebrations—but it is important to try to look after yourself. Meals such as soup or stews, tinned fruit, ice cream, and other foods that don't rely on a lot of digestion tend to be best tolerated. Remember, if you are part of a family, you may be grieving differently. There may be members of the household whose appetites have not been affected. If you are the primary cook, then look at alternatives if you are unable to face cooking. It may be appointing someone else to cook or relying on frozen meals or the occasional takeout (not a problem every now and again, but exercise some caution because it may not be as nutritious as home-cooked food). Look at quick, easy-to-prepare meals, such as pasta and sauce.

If after a few days you find that you are still unable to tolerate a reasonable amount of food, then I would advise you to seek medical help. Medical staff are used to people grieving. You don't have to be embarrassed if you cry. Again, if you are concerned what your doctor might think knowing that your source of grief is an animal companion, just say that a close member of your family has died. You do not have to say anything else.

Sleep

Good, restful sleep can be hard to obtain when grieving, which seems so at odds with your desire to sleep so that you can forget for a few hours. But sometimes, even if you are sleeping for a number of hours, your sleep is disturbed sleep, meaning that you wake up a lot and may have trouble going back to sleep. Sadly, when asleep, you may be plagued by nightmares of your deceased pet or wake up and momentarily forget that they have died.

My suggestions are the common ones: avoid caffeine consumption after dinner (or even from late afternoon). Consider drinking some herbal tea before going to bed if you are missing your caffeine. Make sure you exercise each day, to tire your body. This can be difficult if your main form of exercise was walking your (now deceased) dog. Find ways apart from alcohol to soothe yourself, such as having a hot shower or bubble bath to calm you. Do not have your cell phone, tablet, or computer in the bedroom with you. It is too easy to keep checking emails or to listen for the "ping" of a text. Your mind needs to switch off completely from outside stimuli. If you find you are lying awake, not being able to sleep or get back to sleep, consider getting up and making a warm drink or reading something for half an hour or so.

> *We were so brokenhearted to see him go but he was*
> *in such pain. We couldn't see him suffer. Even now I*
> *sometimes wake up in the night and come out to talk to*
> *him and then remember.*
>
> —Client

My cat sleeps curled up in the crook of my right arm, nestled under my chin. If your deceased animal companion slept on the bed and you are missing their presence, their weight, or bulk, sometimes putting a soft pillow in the gap where they used to sleep or even a soft toy can be of help in inducing sleep. If your cat or dog slept on your feet, having some pressure on top of your feet may trick your brain and body into thinking they are still there and allow you to sleep. Noise or sleep machines may assist too. (Now you can download apps for this. For this activity, you are allowed to have your phone in the bedroom!) If your dog slept beside the bed, don't feel in any rush to move the bedding if it brings you some comfort.

Of course, if you are having trouble sleeping after four days or so, and you have tried various techniques, none of which help, please consider seeking medical advice. You need sleep in order to function.

Daily Routines Change

A client once told me, "I never imagined that losing a pet could hurt so much and our home just isn't the same without him around." And indeed, our much-loved animal companions bring rhythm and provide routine to our lives and to our households. They can be our alarm clocks, our exercise programs, even form part of teams for volunteering, such as being therapy dogs or assistance dogs. They are also our "de-stressors," so without their calming influence, their soulful looks, their humming purrs, life seems pretty bleak and perhaps even too hard.

If you have other pets, some of those items or prompts will probably continue, but, of course, they have altered. You have moved "off center."

How to adapt to this household upheaval? First of all, acknowledge it. There is nothing wrong in admitting that your dog or cat set your routine, perhaps getting you out of bed early each morning.

There is nothing wrong in admitting that you find it hard to exercise, that it isn't as much fun on your own, or that, even if you walk with your partner, your dog brought another dimension to the daily or twice-daily walks. Walking is also about meeting other dog walkers. This can be painful, because you may feel overwhelmed by your dog's absence, upset at the dramatic change in what was once part of your daily routine. Some walkers may ask about the absence of your dog. Even the kindness of others can be hard. Having said that, often other pet owners know just the right words to say, because most of them understand, either having gone through the death of their own animal companions or anticipating how hard it will be for them when that day arrives.

Continuing Guilt

There may be some guilt lying around. Perhaps you feel a sense of relief that an ill one is no longer suffering, but then you remember what that now means—their absence. If you have special photographs taken during their final months, looking at these images, though painful, might make your brain understand what your heart may not: that euthanasia and letting them go was the right course of action.

Looking at photographs of them in their final years may help override the images we are more likely to remember: our animal companion in their younger years. Otherwise ask someone in your household, a close friend, or even your veterinarian for assurance.

Sometimes when we are grieving, we need confirmation from others. The brain is very good at playing games, aided by lack of sleep and a very foggy head.

Navigating Your Way Without Your Beloved One

Healing hearts need time; healing hearts need to be given permission to take each day—even each hour—as it comes.

Be kind to yourself. As I have said before, we only grieve because we love.

So back to the household routines, with some other suggestions.

If you still have another or several animal companions then that probably means you are following a routine, hard though it may be. Even if you have another dog to walk, it isn't the same without your deceased one. Your other dog may find the walk is quite different too, so check on his or her behavior. You may find it helpful to take a different route if you were used to a certain one or two. This may also help your other animal companion, as well as help stem your tears. Driving to a new area or park, seeing different scenery, and meeting other people and their dogs might also be of help.

At home, if their feeding bowls and dishes cause you to tear up, put them away in a cupboard. You may wish to rearrange part of the furniture or the layout of certain rooms. Only do this if you think your other animals will not become distressed by the changes.

It can be hard coming home. If you are working outside the home, you probably looked forward to being greeted by your pet on your return. They may have even been looking out the window for you or sitting by the front door. If you are finding this part of your routine difficult, change it a little. It might mean stopping for a coffee on the way home, shopping for groceries in the evening, perhaps consciously using that time to answer emails, send texts, or have a short read. All of these will break up your routine.

When you get home, if you would normally have walked your dog and do not have any other dogs, sometimes changing into different clothes might give your brain a rest from the strong emotions. Look at small changes you could implement: get into your pajamas, make a hot chocolate, sit down for half an hour before preparing the evening meal, make a phone call. Alter what had been your daily routine; jumble it up. This is a way to give your emotions a rest.

Holidays

Anniversaries are triggers. We acknowledge that the first Christmas, birthday, or wedding anniversary will be hard without our deceased human loved one, but this applies to our animal companions as well.

At Christmas, our pets are often part of the celebration. They may have been part of the "wrapping the presents" party (one of my cats always "helped") or been there to "assist" when decorating the Christmas tree. Many of our animal companions are gift recipients and may have had special food on the day.

People might ask, "What are you going to do this Christmas?" or say, "This will be a difficult Christmas, won't it?" if a human member of the family has died, but they might not make the pet connection.

> *On Boxing Day 2007 we sadly lost our beloved sixteen-year-old cat Oliver due to simple old age. . . . As we don't have children, the loss of Oliver is felt deeper.*
> —Client

Church and secular services are often held just before Christmas (these are sometimes called "Blue Christmas" services), to acknowledge the hardship, the death of a close one, at this special festive time. This is a public acknowledgment of loss and the grief associated with that loss, and it benefits the grieving to gather with others who are grieving. It is harder to "see" pet loss beyond the family; apart from our own family, and perhaps a close friend or two, it is usually a fairly private affair. But attending a service like this can help acknowledge the difficulty during this time.

If your animal companion was part of your Christmas or other holiday celebrations, how can you honor what may be a very sad day? Acknowledgment can be the first step toward preparation. Sometimes buying or making a special Christmas decoration can become a lovely memory. Yes, it is bittersweet, but it is a visible reminder of the invisible. You could buy or craft a decoration in the shape of a dog or cat, or one that functions as a photo frame. Sorting through photographs, choosing a special one for the decoration, can aid healing. Put on some festive music, pour yourself a hot drink, use the good cups (the ones kept in the china cabinet and never used because they are "too good"). Have a good cry if that is what is needed. Your life has changed. As you stretch up to place the decoration on the tree, whisper messages to your deceased pet—tell them how much you love them, how much you miss them, but also try to say that you feel they are with you always, and that they will never be forgotten—always loved.

If you used to purchase a gift for your pet at Christmas time or on their birthdays, consider continuing this tradition with the gift being given to an animal shelter. Contact the shelter first because they may have their own "wish list." Or donate to an animal shelter or animal charity. Giving back can help heal a broken heart, it can lighten the spirit.

What Can Help?

As I have said before, there is no quick or universal way through grief. Each person deals with grief in his or her own way. What may help, though, is the sharing of stories, memories, and photographs. Through the sharing, one often comes to the realization of how blessed or fortunate one has been to have had a wonderful animal companion.

Consider what one client told me: "Alongside our grief is the memory that she brought such joy into our lives, and we are forever grateful we had her for the twelve years she was with us. As you said, some days are better than others. I love to look at the precious photos we have of Missy and remember the times she made us laugh and all the times she allowed us (as only cats can do), to adore her."

Another client said, "Thank you for your card and your beautiful words of wisdom. They have given me great hope and calmness of spirit in dealing with the awful void in my life. My little Jasmine enriched my life, I was very blessed in having her for twelve years. "

Still another wrote, "Speaking to you has helped tremendously, your kindness and wisdom has given me the strength to look beyond the sadness and remember the great memories and love Flossy has given us."

Don't underestimate the power of photographs, the sharing and remembering of stories and antics. Yes, these may be accompanied by tears, but tears are fine! (This is another reason to have a cuppa nearby—to replace the tears!) Perhaps host a special afternoon tea for family and friends, to share stories about your deceased animal companion. Even if you held something similar after you buried your pet at home or scattered their ashes, you can still hold another gathering. There are no set rules to grief, you do what helps you.

In chapter 1, I wrote about the five (or seven) stages of grief. David Kessler, an expert on the subject of grief (he cowrote several books with the late Elisabeth Kübler-Ross), has recently written a book *Finding Meaning: The Sixth Stage of Grief.* Unlike the other additional stages that were added to the original five (shock and testing), Kessler defines the sixth stage of grief as that of finding meaning or hope—indeed, of crafting a way to transform one's life from despair to hope. How do we find meaning again when the one whom we loved so deeply has died? Kessler writes beautifully about how to move toward healing, how to bring that goal into your future. Kessler speaks about making conscious decisions to change, to learn from the death of your loved one.

We must be ready to make this change, though. I caution against doing anything in a hurry or accompanied by the words "I must" or "I should." I am not saying that Kessler says to rush, but I am aware there are voices in our society, maybe even within our own families and among our friends, who say, "You must be nearly over that grief by now," or "It is time for you to get on with your life."

A broken heart is heavy. A broken spirit droops. Exhausted. Please do not rush; attend to things at your own pace, when able. Grief not only breaks; it cripples, and it paralyzes. I believe wisdom comes to you when you are ready and able to receive it. This may be during your darkest hours, when tears flow during the early hours of the morning, or in the blackness of night when you are searching for a glimmer of light. In your pain, you might find healing, hope, meaning, through the balm of a beautiful memory. Perhaps when you consider the strength your pet gave you, you become thankful that your beloved pet changed you, made you a stronger, more compassionate person.

Think about how your animal companion changed you. Have you become more patient? Less judgmental? Are you able to live more in the moment and fret less about the future? In chapter 1, I wrote that our animal companions may become our teachers. Dwell on the gifts given to you. Write them down. Look at them during the next days and weeks, add to them. There may come an answer, a way to utilize or acknowledge some of these gifts. Honor these presents, then start to work out if there is anything you are meant to do with these gifts, apart from living them out as a more patient, trusting, loving person. The answer may lead you to some charitable work or volunteering. If your animal companion died of cancer or from another illness, you may wish to donate to your vet or animal shelter, to help those unable to afford medication or other treatment for their pets, to have their bill partially paid or paid in full. Reflecting on how your pet changed you may cause you to pause or stop to speak with a dog walker about their dog, listening to them air their worries and concerns to another dog lover. As Thornton Wilder is said to have claimed: "The highest tribute to the dead is not grief but gratitude."

What I have found helpful is reflecting on the image of a book. Although your loved animal companion's earthly life has ended, yours has not. Your story continues. The pages that continue may appear to be colorless, even dry and gritty. Sometimes you will find that you return to the page where your loved one died—and it can be hard to move on, to turn the page. Stay with this image for a moment. Do you sense that the book, your life, contains your pet within its pages? If so, then you will always have his or her story held within it. Your pet still travels with you, in an altered form, yes, but his or her spirit, essence, is still there, and it continues to influence you. You will navigate your path along the lines of your continuing story. If you concentrate, you may feel, smell, hear, and see them accompanying you, in a shadowy fashion.

A New Addition

Part of your future story may involve asking the question: When, if ever, should I get another pet? Some literature says you will know when it is the right time. Perhaps, but I am not so sure. We can be so overwhelmed with grief that we feel a new pet will make everything better. Beware! There are good reasons why experts advise those who are grieving *not* to make major life decisions for at least six to twelve months (and getting another pet is a major life decision). The reasons people search for a new animal companion are quite different. We have probably had people tell us that they needed a dog or cat because their house was too quiet or they needed something to come home to.

One client really surprised me in this regard. I had phoned to check on them. Their dog had died a few days before, and they were heartbroken. When I called, I heard a dog barking in the background. The husband told me that he and his wife had sat down to have breakfast the day after their dog had died and realized they had nothing to say to each other. They realized that they always talked to each other about their previous dog, and through their dog—so they rushed out to get another dog, to fill in the marital silence and keep the conversation flowing! I think the new addition was a success.

Sometimes pets appear in our lives when we aren't expecting them, but if you are consciously, deliberately weighing the decision, then take as much time as you need. After a year without my dog Rosa, I went out for a walk. I still went for a morning walk, imagining that she accompanied me in spirit. Now that Rosa was no longer old and blind, she could go as fast as me, and that made my walks easier to bear. I returned home in tears, somehow knowing I was ready for another flesh-and-blood dog. Rosa still accompanies me on her "spirit walks," but she now has dog company, my blind dog, Harry.

I have met people who say they will never get another pet because the grief they felt was just too painful and they never want to go through that trauma again. I understand that, and I respect their decisions. I have also met many who say it hurts so much when they die, but it hurts more to have a pet-free house. They would rather ready themselves for pet death than live a life of loneliness, or emptiness, due to animal absence.

When it comes to adding a new pet, perhaps the conundrum is really "Should I?" not "When should I?" These are two quite different questions, with their own set of answers to satisfy. It is worth taking stock of where you are right now, in this stage of your life. Are you considering moving into a retirement community or renting a different apartment within the next few years? If so, and you are considering getting another pet, you may need to seek out the premises you are interested in, to inquire about their pet policy.

If you are unsure, or uncertain, check your fallback position, especially if you live alone. If something happens to you, who will look after your pet? This is worth considering at any age. We live in uncertain times, and it does give peace of mind knowing that, if something happens to you, your loved one will be taken care of in a loving home. Provisions need to be made—for both parties.

If you feel you are unable to take on another pet, then this may indeed be particularly hard to bear. This, too, is grief. I have met people who say that they are too old to take on that responsibility, or feel that getting a pet may make them more liable to have a fall. Perhaps they struggle to bend down, so are unable to change the litter box or pick up after their animal companion. Again, check your family and friend situation. If you feel you are unable to live without a cat or dog, check what services can be drawn on for assistance. There may be a voluntary group or animal organization in your area that offers services so that people can keep a pet. This might be achieved by assisting with dog walking, changing litter, feeding, et cetera. If you are unable to, or feel it would be irresponsible to have another animal companion, you might consider visiting a friend with a pet, or visiting an animal shelter or even a cat café to get an animal "fix."

Sometimes it doesn't seem like a home without an animal. There are lifelike toys of cats, that are covered in fur, that have some movement, and even purr, that may ease the grief. These have been used quite successfully in aged-care settings.

> *When emotions have settled and the timing is just right, I will be back to adopt yet another family member. I think Evie [cat] really needs the company, and nothing makes me happier than a house that purrs.*
> —Client

If you have other animal companions, think carefully about what would suit them. If you have an elderly animal companion, perhaps a puppy or kitten would be too boisterous, too bouncy, too unsettling for them. Some pets prefer to be on their own. If you are going to introduce a new animal companion, consider steps to be taken. Talk to your vet or your local animal shelter about ways to introduce new animals. Have a spare room in which you can keep the new addition as your other pet(s) adjust, knowing there is a new creature in the house. Sometimes products are used to dispense calming smells. Be armed with information and strategies. For the majority of cases, most animals take time to settle. Be prepared for hostility. If you are not prepared for these stresses, then that is your answer!

There is nothing wrong with *not* being ready. It is better—better for you, and better for the animals—to know that than to face possible problems. Remember, a family is made up of individuals with very different personalities; the same applies to our blended pet families. Don't expect your fifteen-year-old cat to welcome a new dog. Your cat may have tolerated or been friends with your previous dog because the dog had accepted that the cat was part of the household before the dog came. The dog understood the pecking order. Time can change things, but be prepared for the long haul and make sure you have the energy to bring to the task. Additions take time and energy: make sure you have both.

Do not consider a new addition until you feel you are not in danger of making comparisons. Every animal is different. All members of the family have to be on board for this, otherwise what should be a wonderful experience could be fraught with failure before the animal has time to adjust to their new living arrangements.

Do not expect your new pet to do or like the same things as your previous animal companion. It takes time for a pet to settle into its new home and environment, so give them space—and time. Sometimes it can be helpful if your new addition's gender is the opposite of the previous one and it's a different color, to help thwart comparisons. Do not go looking for a "lookalike." You will be sorely disappointed (as will the new pet), and you are setting yourself up for disappointment.

But when your heart is open and you are prepared, a new pet can mean another opportunity to love. Consider these haiku I wrote after adopting Harry.

> *I am in love.*
> *New dog glued to me—I count*
> *licks, not syllables.*

> *Dog kisses at dawn*
> *make up for lack of sleep.*
> *A day of promise.*

Resources to Help When Acquiring Another Pet

There are a number of picture books that address this topic, one being *The Best Cat in the World* by Leslea Newman. In the story, Charlie, an elderly male ginger cat, dies. Victor, the boy, grieves deeply, has trouble eating, and cries a lot. The family buries Charlie in the backyard, and plants a rosebush that resembles Charlie, because it has orange flowers, the color of Charlie's fur, and green leaves, the color of Charlie's eyes. After a number of weeks, the vet phones to tell Victor's mother that there is a kitten that needs a home. They go to meet the kitten. It is a female tortoiseshell with different colored fur and eyes. This kitten doesn't do the same things that Charlie did. She has her own ways of playing and eating. She even cuddles differently and prefers to sleep on the windowsill, not next to Victor, like Charlie did. At the end of the story, Victor and the kitten look out the window at Charlie's rosebush. Victor asks: "Who's the best cat in the world?" a question he would ask Charlie at the end of each day. The new kitten purred a reply, as Charlie once did.

The book addresses how to live with a new animal companion while not forgetting the deceased one. It also touches on the feeling of guilt caused by "replacing" the deceased pet. Having another pet does not erase the feelings you have for your deceased animal companion and the joy you experienced in the life you shared. These precious memories and love continue to enrich your life; they give it both depth and meaning.

There are a number of other children's picture books that address this issue, often with the deceased animal initiating the meeting between the grieving person or family and the new addition. These books affirm that life goes on and make the assumption that their deceased pet would not be jealous but rather would be glad that another animal has found a loving home. Most of the stories bring in the element of remembrance. Just because an animal companion has died doesn't mean the deceased has been forgotten. These narratives add an element of hope, of meaning, of showing us that life goes on, and although we have changed, there will come a time when we will experience joy or happiness again. Alongside this change we are gently reminded that we won't forget our deceased animal companion, and that we should not feel guilty if we bring home a new addition.

It is important enough to note again: the word *replaced* should not be said or implied when introducing a new pet into the household. No dog, cat, bird, or rabbit can be replaced.

Further Help

As I have said throughout this book, if you are finding life difficult, overwhelming, or oppressive, please seek professional help. Either visit your healthcare provider or make contact with a qualified grief counselor. If the grief counselor does not specialize in pet loss, he or she should be able to refer you to someone who does. Do not be embarrassed asking for help. You are grieving the loss of a loved one. It can be helpful to acknowledge one's feelings and to talk to someone who understands.

Many of my previous clients have found being listened to, supported, and validated to be of help. Surely we can do that for another. We can be kind, gentle, patient, and loving, qualities our animal companions forged in us. Perhaps we can imagine we are doctors, listening with the stethoscope of care and compassion to the grieving heart. We are connected, we remain connected, with our deceased animal companions, and with one another. Love continues.

An elderly New Yorker once asked her dying husband how she was going to survive without him. He pronounced these inspiring words: "Take the love you have for me and spread it around." May we go and do likewise, in memory of our much-loved, precious animal companions.

> *I do miss both my pets terribly. And although I don't*
> *feel I took them for granted, it really is only when*
> *they're gone that you realize how much you rely on them*
> *being there. I know they will always stay with me in*
> *my heart.*
>
> —Client

CONCLUSION

BROKEN HEARTS. SHATTERED hearts. Your heart.

When something has broken, and later is mended, the repair is never perfect.

But do you really want perfect? Perfection? Perfect implies no death, but also no deep and sustaining memories that make up your very being, help form who you are. Rabbi Menachem Mendel of Kotzk (1787–1859) said, "There is nothing more whole than a broken heart."

Your heart is now a mosaic, consisting of the chambers of spiritual, buried, young, and shattered. You may even imagine a kaleidoscope of colors accompanying each chamber. The glue that holds your heart together is memory: the memories of your beloved pet.

If you look closely at your stuck-back-together heart, you will notice some gaps, edges that are not flush, or perhaps a jagged shard, standing alone, a sentry, out of place. During the days and years to come, some of these "gaps" will be filled in, shards repaired or filed down. This healing may come courtesy of a once-forgotten memory, now recovered, or via a friend's reminiscence, or perhaps seeing the chewed dog ball, discovered at the bottom of the garden when clearing the autumn leaves, or, when opening a book, finding the cat whisker that had been placed between its pages for safe keeping.

Your imperfect heart continues to beat. When grief's shadow threatens to overwhelm you, it may skip a beat. This palpitation may occur gently, such as on a crisp winter's morning that reminds you of your brisk walks together, when fog and breath mingled. Interesting that these palpitations, these "skipped beats," have been described by medical practitioners as "fluttery," "throbbing," "pounding," "flip-flopping," and "murmuring." I love that last word. Doesn't our deceased keep "murmuring" to us?

Look closely at your heart. It is broken, shattered, but not destroyed. It has changed. Its covering seems to shine, even sparkle. You only get a shine like that from the combination of two ingredients: tears and love.

Your heart will never be as it was; you know you will never be as before. Yet in time, I hope you will be able to feel the gift that your much-loved animal companion's passing has been in your life. All grief alters us, reminds us that our earthly lives will end, but the loss of a pet may bless us with the difficult spiritual lessons of living in the moment, coated with the teaching of unconditional love.

Learning to live in the present can be a difficult lesson, but a treasure if embraced, for moments are all we have. Our pets lived in the moment. They did not fret about the past or worry about the future. They embraced the joy of the present. When you entered the room or arrived home, they greeted you with an exuberance that was special. Even when they were elderly and could no longer jump or dance their delight as before, their hearts still rejoiced that you had come home. You were with them. You had returned.

Moments. Love-encrusted finite morsels of time.

These moments are your heart's glue. You carry your loved one with you every day, for eternity. You no longer hold them in your arms or stoke them in their beds. Instead, they are held deep within your heart, remembered, and loved forever.

You are richer, blessed for having them as part of your family.

Rabbi David J. Wolpe wrote, along the lines of Rabbi Menachem Mendel: "The only whole heart is a broken one because it lets the light in." A whole heart, an unshattered heart, does not have the capacity to let in light. It has no cracks, no memory glue. Within its perfection there is no opportunity to hear the echo of a bark, or remember the fragrance of a wet dog, or feel the plonk of a cat as they settle on your lap.

May the glue of your memories let in the light, the sound of laughter, and joy, which will lighten your soul and spirit. Listen to your heart, because "only the heart knows how to find what is precious."

In Willie Morris's book, *My Dog Skip*, he writes about the death of his boyhood friend, Skip: "They had buried him under our elm tree, they said—yet this was not totally true. For he really lay buried in my heart."

NOTES

Introduction

1 ***"to the dogs who have gone ahead"":*** Garth Nix, *Frogkisser!* (Crows Nest, NSW: Allen & Unwin, 2017).

3 ***Death had entered the world:*** Roy Willis, ed., *World Mythology: The Illustrated Guide* (London: Duncan Baird, 1993), 224.

4 ***"This sorrow I feel is great":*** Thomas George, "Coyote and His Beautiful Daughter," in *Coyote Tales of the Northwest* (Edmonton: Eschia Books, 2010), 182–83.

6 ***So in Hebrew, dog means:*** Jonathan Wittenberg, *Things My Dog Has Taught Me* (London: Hodder & Stoughton, 2018), 205–6.

6 ***The word for puppy:*** Rabbi Mark Joel Mahler, "The Light at Death's Door: Achare-Kedoshim Leviticus 16:1–20:27," *Pittsburgh Jewish Chronicle*, April 29, 2009, https://jewishchronicle.timesofisrael.com/the-light-at-deaths-doorachare-kedoshim-leviticus-161-2027.

Heartbeat

7 ***Freud loved Lun Yu:*** Stanley Coren writes the dog's name as "Lun Yug" whereas others pen it as "Lun Yu."

7 ***Anna made her father's birthday:*** Stanley Coren, *The Pawprints of History: Dogs and the Course of Human Events* (New York: Free Press/Simon & Schuster, 2003), 137.

7 ***It was noted that Jofi:*** Coren, *The Pawprints of History*, 139.

8 ***"Apart from any mourning":*** Susie Green, "Freud's Dream Companions," *The Guardian*, March 23, 2002, https://www.theguardian.com/theguardian/2002/mar/23/weekend7.weekend3.

Chapter 1

10   ***the deep suffering Coyote felt:*** George, "Coyote and His Beautiful Daughter," 182–83.

11   ***When the same industry group did their first survey:*** American Pet Products Association, "Pet Industry Market Size, Trends, & Ownership Statistics," accessed August 8, 2023, https://www.americanpetproducts.org/press_industrytrends.asp.

11   ***In Australia, where I live:*** Hallie Roddy, "10 Australia Pet Ownership Statistics to Know in 2023: How Many Pets Are in Australia?" PetKeen, last updated July 6, 2023, https://petkeen.com/australia-pet-ownership-statistics/#General_Australian_Pet_Statistics.

11   ***In 2022, UK pet ownership:*** Tim Wall, "UK Pet Ownership at 62 percent Overall in 2022, Dogs Top List," PetFoodIndustry.com, May 15, 2022, https://www.petfoodindustry.com/articles/11288-uk-pet-ownership-at-62-overall-in-2022-dogs-top-list.

11   ***a sharp rise from its 2011–12:*** Braemar Finance Blog, "Facts & Figures: Pet Ownership," November 8, 2021, https://www.braemarfinance.co.uk/news-and-insights/facts-figures-pet-ownership.

13   ***Argos then dies:*** Homer, *Odyssey*, Book 17.

14   ***In 2005, a burial plot of a man:*** University of Cambridge, "Was the Fox Prehistoric Man's Best Friend?" Phys.org.com, January 27, 2011, https://phys.org/news/2011-01-fox-prehistoric-friend.html; Lisa A. Maher, Jay T. Stock, Sarah Finney, James J. N. Heywood, Preston T. Miracle, and Edward B. Banning, "A Unique Human–Fox Burial from a Pre-Natufian Cemetery in the Levant (Jordan)," *PlosOne* 6, no. 1 (2011): e15815, https://doi.org/10.1371/journal.pone.0015815.

17   ***For those whose dogs were their own assisted-therapy dogs:*** Although slightly outside the scope of this book, it is important to remember that grief extends to the death of an animal

not classed as a "pet"; these include dogs trained and utilized by the military, police, and drug-detecting agencies (maybe even animals in zoos and circuses). Trainers form strong bonds with their four-legged working colleagues, and the grief experienced when a dog has died, or has been retired and moved elsewhere, needs to be acknowledged. Many of these organizations do seek professional help for the grieving trainer/colleagues following the death/move of a working dog.

20 ***Theologian Joan Chittister writes:*** Joan Chittister, *Gospel Days* (Maryknoll, NY: Orbis Books, 1999), 139.

20 ***Or, as Winnie the Pooh put it:*** This quote is probably misattributed to A. A. Milne.

22 ***In the 1970s, Elisabeth Kübler-Ross set out:*** Elisabeth Kübler-Ross, *On Death and Dying* (London: Tavistock Publications, 1970).

22 ***According to Kübler-Ross:*** David Kessler wrote about the sixth stage of grief in *Finding Meaning: The Sixth Stage of Grief* (London: Rider/Penguin Random House, 2019). I will write about the sixth stage of grief in chapter 5.

33 ***Use social media, plus old-fashioned posters:*** The book *Lost: Lost and Found Pet Posters from around the World* by Ian Phillips (New York: Princeton Architectural Press, 2002) is both a sad read and a testament to our love of pets. The book highlights what *may* be cultural differences: "One letter from someone in Iceland explained that people in Iceland don't lose their pets and that I would never get a poster from anyone there. Another letter from the Netherlands told me 'We just don't do that sorta thing in Holland. Lose a pet and the thing to do is to go out and buy a new one. . .,'" from the book's introduction (no page numbers). I wonder what a recent survey would reveal?

40 ***"I'll tell you when you get back."***:*The Friendship Book, 2022* (London: D. C. Thomson, 2022), 141.

Heartbeat

41   *"My best friend, my dog Jennie, has died.'":* Selma G. Lanes, *The Art of Maurice Sendak* (New York: Abradale Press/Harry N. Abrams, 1993), 151.

41   *These are all minor roles really:* Maurice Sendak, *Higglety Pigglety Pop! or There Must Be More to Life* (London: The Bodley Head, 1967).

42   *"Sendak said: 'It was all a nightmare'":* Lanes, *The Art of Maurice Sendak*, 153.

42   *After several adventures:* Talking about preparing for a journey, needing to pack their bags, is a common theme among the dying. "The notion of the dying preparing for a journey isn't new or unusual . . . it's always referring to an earthly journey. . . . The archetype is about life and transitions, not endings." David Kessler, *Visions, Trips, and Crowded Rooms* (New York: Hay House, 2010), xx–xxi.

43   *"I can't tell you how to get to the Castle Yonder'":* Sendak, *Higglety Pigglety Pop!*, 69.

43   *In an earlier version, Sendak added:* Lanes, *The Art of Maurice Sendak*, 167.

43   *Sendak wrote a libretto for an opera:* Knussen had not completed the musical composition at the time the opera was first performed. It took another thirteen years before the musical score was finished. Tony Kushner, *The Art of Maurice Sendak: 1980 to the Present* (New York: Harry N. Abrams, 2003), 144.

43   *Tony Kushner believes that the book:* Kushner, *The Art of Maurice Sendak*, 144.

43   *"Jennie was the love of my life,'":* Lanes, *The Art of Maurice Sendak*, 156.

43   *Many of us can identify with Sendak:* Lanes, 171.

Chapter 2

47 *if the late Rev. Billy Graham can say:* Billy Graham, "Billy Graham: You Very Well Could See Your Pets in Heaven," *Seattle Pi* (The Seattle Post-Intelligencer), September 21, 2003, https://www.seattlepi.com/news/article/Billy-Graham-You-very-well-could-see-your-pets-1123692.php; Billy Graham, "Answers," Billy Graham Evangelistic Association, January 24, 2013, https://billygraham.org/answer/i-suppose-youve-been-asked-this-before-but-will-there-be-animals-in-heaven.

48 *This one, attributed to St. Basil:* Attributed to St. Basil (d. 379 CE), cited in Charles Birch, "Respect for Animals," in Charles Birch and Lukas Vischer, *Living with the Animals: The Community of God's Creatures* (Geneva: World Council of Churches, 1997), 59. Adapted from a prayer devised in 1915 by Arthur Winnington-Ingram, bishop of London.

49 *To use the word* animal*:* Barbara Allen, *Animals in Religion* (London: Reaktion Books, 2016), 52.

50 *Wesley was convinced:* Daniel Hahn, *The Tower Menagerie* (London: Pocket Books, 2004), 1–3.

50 *We may as well deny that they have sight or hearing:* The Wesley Center Online at Northwest Nazarene University, The Sermons of John Wesley—Sermon 60, "The General Deliverance," accessed August 8, 2023, http://wesley.nnu.edu/john-wesley/the-sermons-of-john-wesley-1872-edition/sermon-60-the-general-deliverance. I have also consulted Andrew Linzey and Tom Regan, eds., *Animals and Christianity: A Book of Readings* (London: Crossroad Publishing, 1989), 102–3, and used their punctuation.

50 *"In the new earth":* Linzey and Regan, *Animals and Christianity*.

50 *One congregant wrote:* William Raeper, *George MacDonald* (Tring: Lion Publishing, 1987), 90.

51 *I know of no reason why:* George MacDonald, *Hope of the Gospel,* Project Gutenberg edition, 2004, https://www.gutenberg.org/files/14453/14453-h/14453-h.htm.

51 *C. S. Lewis's view diverged:* Lewis credited MacDonald as being his master: "I have never concealed the fact that I regarded him as my master; indeed I fancy I have never written a book in which I did not quote from him," in *George MacDonald: An Anthology,* ed. C. S. Lewis (Glasgow: Collins Fount, 1983), xxxii.

51 *The error we must avoid:* C. S. Lewis, *The Problem of Pain* (London: Collins Fontana Books, 4th imp., 1962), 126–27.

52 *The United Methodist website advocates caring for animals:* Churchmouse Campanologist, "Apologetics Corner: Animals and Heaven," May 11, 2011, https://churchmousec.wordpress.com/2011/05/11/apologetics-corner-animals-and-heaven/.

52 *"In his blogpost 'All Dogs Go to Heaven,'":* Frederick W. Schmidt, "All Dogs Go to Heaven," *United Methodist Insight,* October 28, 2019, https://um-insight.net/in-the-church/practicing-faith/%E2%80%9Call-dogs-go-to-heaven%E2%80%9D/.

52 *"'All dogs go to heaven,'":* Schmidt, "All Dogs Go to Heaven."

53 *According to Vatican Radio, the pope had said:* Jim Atkin, "Did Pope Francis Say Animals Go to Heaven?" *National Catholic Register,* December 13, 2014, https://www.ncregister.com/blog/did-pope-francis-say-animals-go-to-heaven.

53 *They had been spoken by a previous pope:* David Stout, "Pope Francis Says There's a Place for Pets in Paradise," *Time,* December 12, 2014, https://time.com/3631242/pope-francis-dogs-heaven-catholic-church.

55 *In the Talmud, it is stated that:* Jerusalem Talmud Ketubot 4:8—within the context of the marriage contract (*ketubah*) and family law, rather than animal welfare.

55 *"'[I]t is not appropriate to incorporate our traditional mourning'":* Rabbi Janet Offel, "When a Beloved Pet Dies," accessed August 8, 2023, https://merrimackvalleyhavurah.wordpress.com

/2022/12/20/a-jewish-way-to-mourn-a-pets-loss/. "El Maleh Rahamim" ("God full of compassion") is a Jewish prayer for the deceased which is recited at funeral services, when visiting the graves of relatives, and on the anniversary of the death of a close relative. It is said on other occasions too.

56 *A modern example would be praying:* Karen Iris Tucker, "Mourning for Pets, the 'Jewish' Way?" *Haaretz*, April 29, 2012, https://www.haaretz.com/jewish/2012-04-29/ty-article/mourning-for-pets-the-jewish-way/0000017f-e911-df2c-a1ff-ff51d2140000.

58 *"I carefully put my hand over his eyes'":* Jonathan Wittenberg, *Things My Dog Has Taught Me About Being a Better Human* (London: Hodder & Stoughton, 2018), 198.

58 *The vet proceeded to administer:* Wittenberg, *Things My Dog Has Taught Me*, 198.

58 *If God is love, and present in all the love there is:* Wittenberg, 201–2.

59 *"'To God bow all creatures of the heavens and the earth'":* *The Koran*, trans. N. J. Dawood (London: Penguin, 2006), 190.

59 *Some Mu'tazilites, who were a school of Islamic theologians:* Mu'tazilites were a radical school of Islamic theologians prominent in the early ninth century. Richard Foltz, *Animals in Islamic Tradition and Muslim Cultures* (Oxford: Oneworld Academic, 2006), 6.

59 *One Mu'tazilite theologian, Abu Ishaq an-Nazzam:* Foltz, *Animals in Islamic Tradition and Muslim Cultures*, 7.

59 *One, Muhammad ibn Jarir-al-Tabari:* Ibn Jarir al-Tabari, *Jami al-bayan an ta wil al-Qur an* (Beirut: Dar al-Kutub al-'Ilmiyyah, 1999), vol. 5, 186; cited in Sarra Tlili, "All Animals Are Equal, or Are They? The Ikhwan al-Safa's Animal Epistle and Its Unhappy End" (unpublished article, 2011), 8.

60 *The Qur'anic verse, "No creature is there crawling on the earth":* In some versions of the Qur'an, "mustered" has been translated as "gathered."

60   ***Some of these may be cultural:*** Dogs in Islam," Animals in Islam (website), accessed August 8, 2023, https://www.animalsinislam.com/islam-animal-rights/dogs.

60   ***The 'M,' which can be seen on tabby cats:*** In a Christian version, a cat jumps into the manger, and its purring stops the baby Jesus from crying. A very grateful Mary pats the cat; the mark from her fingers on its forehead forms an "M" for "Mary."

60   ***Rather, the question is more along the lines of:*** Although Jainism falls under this heading, it won't form part of the discussion. Jainism discourages the keeping of pets, because of the difficulty of sustaining them on vegetarian food (and thereby indirectly contributing to the meat industry). It is a Jainist precept that no one should kill any form of life. Among some adherents of Jainism there is an understanding that if one keeps a pet, one is interfering with their natural way of being.

61   ***This means that the animal soul is not regarded as inferior:*** Jayaram V, "The Significance of Animals in Hinduism," Hinduwebsite.com, accessed August 8, 2023, https://www.hinduwebsite.com/hinduism/h_animals.asp.

61   ***In the Vedic tradition, a human has two births:*** Jayaram V, "The Significance of Animals in Hinduism."

61   ***In Hinduism, there is some uncertainty:*** Jayaram V.

62   ***According to Buddhist writer David Michie:*** David Michie, *Buddhism for Pet Lovers: Supporting Our Closest Companions through Life and Death* (Sydney: Allen & Unwin, 2017), 157. I am indebted to Michie for his sensitive explanation of Buddhist beliefs and practices surrounding death and dying, and how these relate to our animal companions.

62   ***Michie advocates natural death because it allows the animal:*** Michie, *Buddhism for Pet Lovers*, 159.

62   ***Michie writes that if it is karma:*** Michie, 160.

63   ***"How will they cope with an abrupt physical and mental dissolution":*** Michie, 160.

64 ***For pets, Michie suggests that their belongings:*** Michie, 165.

64 ***During this seven-week period, each week:*** Michie, 164.

65 ***"Yudhishthira replies, 'This dog, O Lord of the Past and the Present'":*** Barbara Allen, *Animals in Religion* (London: Reaktion Books, 2016), 322. This tale is from the *Mahabharata* 17.2–3. The retelling of it comes from Jeffrey Moussaieff Masson, *Dogs Never Lie About Love* (London: Vintage, 1998), 187–88, which is from his own translation of the original Sanskrit. It is retold in Jean Houston's *Mystical Dogs* (Maui: Inner Ocean, 2002), with several changes. In Liz Rosenberg's poem, "Elegy for a Beagle Mutt," *The Missouri Review* 6, no. 1 (Fall 1982): 29, she writes "and I stay here, reminded of the Buddhist saint who waited at the gates of heaven ten thousand years with his faithful dog, till both were permitted in." Thanks to Jeffrey Moussaieff Masson's footnote about this poem. Does it matter if its origin is Hindu or Buddhist?

65 ***At this point, the dog reveals himself:*** Allen, *Animals in Religion*, 322.

65 ***And the great king and his dog entered Paradise:*** Houston, *Mystical Dogs*, 3.

67 ***Just this side of heaven is a place called Rainbow Bridge:*** For this version and more on various claims of authorship, see "Rainbow Bridge: Pet Story and Poem," History of Bridges (website), accessed August 8, 2023, http://www.historyofbridges.com/mythological-bridges/rainbow-bridge-pets.

67 ***There is uncertainty concerning the authorship:*** See also Paul C. Dahm, *The Rainbow Bridge* (Running Tide Press, 1998); William N. Britton, *The Legend of Rainbow Bridge* (Savannah Publishing, 1994); and Wallace Sife, *The Loss of a Pet* (New Jersey: Howell Book House, 2005). In my edition, which is the third edition, the reflection/poem can be found on pages 215–16. Another contender is a Scottish writer and artist, Edna Clyne-Reky, who is said to have written the poem in the mid-1970s after the death of her son's dog; see Ronnie Casey, "Rainbow Bridge

Remembrance Day," Redbluff Daily News, August 27, 2021, https://www.redbluffdailynews.com/2021/08/27/rainbow-bridge-remembrance-day.

67 ***"Like 'Footprints' or 'Footprints in the Sand,'":*** There are a number of contenders, including Margaret Fishback Powers, Burrell Webb, Carolyn Carty, and Mary Stevenson. Stevenson claimed to have written it in 1939, and proof of authenticity was granted to her on May 3, 1997, but this has not stopped litigation claims; see Rachel Aviv, "Enter Sandman," Poetry Foundation (website), accessed August 8, 2023, https://www.poetryfoundation.org/articles/68974/enter-sandman.

68 ***"'Do dogs go to heaven?' I asked":*** Margaret Marshall Saunders, *Beautiful Joe's Paradise, or The Island of Brotherly Love* (Boston: L. C. Page, 1902; reprint London: Forgotten Books, 2018), 15.

69 ***I caught my breath:*** Marshall Saunders, *Beautiful Joe's Paradise*, 22.

69 ***Some have hypothesized that the Rainbow Bridge:*** The etymology of the name has been contested. In its original form, "Bilröst" can be translated as "the fleetingly glimpsed rainbow." The old Norse word *bil* means "a moment," so "fleeting nature" would fit. The more modern "Bifröst" translates to mean "the shaking or trembling rainbow." The old Norse word *bifa*, "to shake or shimmer," is connected to Bifröst, so it could mean "a shimmering" or "swaying" road to heaven.

70 ***According to veterinarian, author, and animal advocate Dr. Michael W. Fox:*** Cited in Michael W. Fox, "Animal Spirits: Companion Animal Communications after Death," accessed September 18, 2023, https://drfoxonehealth.com/post/animal-spirits-companion-animal-communications-after-death/.

71 ***Some psychics have written books about what happens:*** One example is Karen A. Anderson's book *The Amazing Afterlife of Animals: Messages and Signs from Our Pets on the Other Side* (United States: Painted Rain Publishing, 2017).

71 ***One such account goes like this:*** David Sunfellow, "Kenneth
Ring: Do Our Pets Have an Afterlife?" The Formula for Creating
Heaven on Earth (website), September 27, 2001, https://the-
formula.org/kenneth-ring-do-our-pets-have-an-afterlife/.

Heartbeat

73 ***How pleasant to know Mr Lear!:*** From the poem/song "How
Pleasant to Know Mr Lear!" by Edward Lear. Lear called it the
"Self-Portrait of the Laureate of Nonsense." The last line in
the quote is about Lear, but it could also describe Foss's ample
physique.

73 ***This was due to a superstition:*** Susan Chitty, *That Singular Person Called Lear* (Stroud: Tempus Publishing, 2007), 250.

74 ***Foss became much loved:*** Vivien Noakes, *Edward Lear* (London: Ariel Books/BBC, 1985), 213. This note comes from Lear's
diary, the date being February 23, 1873.

74 ***As Foss aged, he became quite rotund:*** Chitty, *That Singular
Person Called Lear*, 280.

74 ***Lear and Foss were at a sitting:*** Lady Strachey, ed., *Later Letters
of Edward Lear* (London: T. Fisher Unwin, 1911), 361.

74 ***"Foss is dead":*** Vivien Noakes, ed., *Edward Lear: Selected Letters* (Oxford: Oxford University Press, 1990), 282. In Strachey's
Later Letters of Edward Lear, the date of Foss's death is in a letter
dated September 29, not November 29. I have tended to err on
the side of later scholarship (Noakes, Chitty, and Levi), yet Jenny
Uglow, in *Mr Lear: A Life of Art and Nonsense* (London: Faber &
Faber, 2017), 519, writes that Foss died in early September, and
in *Edward Lear: The Life of a Wanderer* (London: Collins, 1968),
Vivien Noakes writes that Lear returned to San Remo in September and "A few days later Foss, his last faithful companion,
died," 311. September or November? Lear was confused at the
time, and was suffering from depression, so dates may have been
incorrectly written on letters and in his diary.

75 **Beneath this stone was buried . . . my good cat Foss***:* Noakes, *Edward Lear: Selected Letters*, 283.

75 ***Lear had him buried in the garden:*** Peter Levi, *Edward Lear: A Biography* (London: Macmillan, 1995), 330.

75 ***In Lear's final letter:*** Noakes, *Edward Lear: Selected Letters*, 283.

Chapter 3

84 ***If you don't want to start from scratch:*** Warren Hanson, *Paw Prints in the Stars* (North Golden Valley: Tristan Publishing, 2008). At the time of writing, this journal was still available.

84 ***"It doesn't mean our love is being put away":*** Hanson, *Paw Prints in the Stars*, no page number.

85 ***Books can be an entry point:*** Although I do not mention books for older children/teenagers, there are many that touch on this topic, from the classics of *Black Beauty* (Anna Sewell), *Thomasina* (Paul Gallico), and *Charlotte's Web* (E. B. White), to *Each Little Bird That Sings* (Deborah Wiles). Books for older readers may allude to pet death. Picture books tend to telescope the topic, whereas fiction for older readers may have pet/animal death as part of the narrative, rather than the story addressing it as the main or sole issue. I write about picture books because they are usually fairly easily to access, and most are appropriate for all ages. Ask older children/teenagers if they have read a book/ watched a movie where there has been a death of a pet/animal? How did they feel? How was it addressed? How would they have altered it/written it?

87 ***Lilah, continuing to chase the cat, climbs up the tree:*** Edwina Wyatt, *Olive* (Richmond, Vic.: Little Hare/Hardie Grant, 2021).

87 ***One story,* Missing Jack *by Rebecca Elliott:*** Rebecca Elliott, *Missing Jack* (Oxford: Lion Children's/Lion Hudson, 2015).

96 ***It takes some time for Zack to grasp this:*** Patrice Karst, *The Invisible Leash* (New York: Little, Brown, 2019), 13.

Heartbeat

101 ***A small pet is often an excellent companion for the sick or long chronic cases:*** Florence Nightingale, *Notes on Nursing, What It IS and What It Is Not* (London: Harrison & Sons, 1859), 58; sighted in Joy Schiller, "Nightingale's Cats," accessed August 9, 2023, https://www.countryjoe.com/nightingale/cats.htm.

102 ***At the Nightingale residence, Athena would perch:*** Ellen McDonald, "An Owl for a Nightingale," *Irish Daily Mail*, March 28, 2018, https://www.pressreader.com/ireland/irish-daily-mail/20180328/282059097549866.

102 ***According to her sister, Parthenope:*** *Florence Nightingale's Pet Owl, ATHENA: A Sentimental History by Parthenope, Lady Verney* (limited edition, San Francisco: Graghorn-Hoyem Press, 1970), accessed August 9, 2023, https://www.countryjoe.com/nightingale/athena.htm.

102 ***"She looked upon Athena as a great great niece'":*** *Florence Nightingale's Pet Owl, ATHENA.*

103 ***"Every meal she considered to have been brought for her especial use'":*** *Florence Nightingale's Pet Owl, ATHENA.*

103 ***Athena perished in the attic:*** There are some differences in accounts, but neglect seems to have been the major cause of Athena's death.

104 ***"Athena came along the cliff quite to my feet'":*** Elaine Mansfield, "An Uncommon Caregiver: Florence Nightingale's Feathered Nursing Assistant," elainemansfield.com, March 10, 2015, https://elainemansfield.com/2015/uncommon-caregiver-florence-nightingales-feathered-nursing-assistant.

Chapter 4

107 ***When Adam saw this, he did the same:*** *Pirke de-Rabbi Eliezer* 21, cited in David Goldstein, *Jewish Mythology* (London: Hamlyn, 1988), 8.

108 ***Back in 2011, nearly six hundred animal graves:*** Archaeo-zoologist Marta Osypinska and her team discovered the grave-yard in 2011. David Grimm, "Graves of Nearly 600 Cats and Dogs in Ancient Egypt May Be World's Oldest Pet Ceme-tery," science.org, February 26, 2021, https://www.science.org/content/article/graves-nearly-600-cats-and-dogs-ancient-egypt-may-be-world-s-oldest-pet-cemetery.

109 ***The majority were cats:*** Of the 585 animals excavated, 536 were cats, and there were thirty-two dogs, fifteen monkeys, one fox, and one falcon. Laura Geggel, "World's Oldest Pet Cemetery Discovered in Ancient Egypt?" livescience.com, March 8, 2021, https://www.livescience.com/oldest-pet-cemetery-ancient-egypt.html.

110 ***The site contains the grave of a dog:*** Gemma Tarlach, "Is This Egyptian Site the World's Oldest Pet Cemetery? Perhaps, But Humans All over the World, from Siberia to Illinois, Have a Long History of Burying Animals with Respect," atlasobscura.com, March 4, 2021, https://www.atlasobscura.com/articles/oldest-pet-cemetery-berenice-egypt.

110 ***Losey affirms this claim:*** Tarlach, "Is This Egyptian Site the World's Oldest Pet Cemetery?"

110 ***In 2015, New York passed a law:*** Lynne Wallis, "A Short History of Pet Cemeteries," *Reader's Digest*, May 10, 2021, https://www.readersdigest.co.uk/inspire/life/a-short-history-of-pet-cemeteries.

110 ***It was established in Hyde Park:*** Wallis, "A Short History of Pet Cemeteries." Sources differ on Cherry's gender.

110 ***It was a spot the dog loved:*** Andrew Day, "Hyde Park Secret Pet Cemetery," Historic UK, accessed August 9, 2023, https://www.historic-uk.com/HistoryMagazine/DestinationsUK/Hyde-Park-Secret-Pet-Cemetery.

110 ***Cherry's tiny tombstone reads:*** Day, "Hyde Park Secret Pet Cemetery."

111 ***The PDSA provided a meadow in its grounds:*** Marie Carter Robb, "Remembering the British 'Pet Holocaust': WW2's Slaughtered Cats and Dogs," *The Independent*, November 12, 2017, https://www.independent.co.uk/news/long_reads/world-war-two-pet-slaughter-death-cats-dogs-a8042026.html. For more information, see Clare Campbell, *Bonzo's War: Animals under Fire 1939–1945* (London: Corsair, 2013), and Hilda Keen, *The Great Cat & Dog Massacre* (Chicago: University of Chicago Press, 2017).

112 ***At this time, in response to public health laws:*** Edward C. Martin III, *The Peaceable Kingdom in Hartsdale: America's First Pet Cemetery* (independently published, 2013), 13.

112 ***The cost of a plot was not cheap:*** Martin, *The Peaceable Kingdom in Hartsdale*, 15.

113 **He came into my life:** Edward C. Martin Jr., *Dr Johnson's Apple Orchard: The Story of America's First Pet Cemetery* (New York: Hartsdale Canine Cemetery, 1997), 40.

113 **The only sorrow you ever brought me:** Martin, *Dr Johnson's Apple Orchard*, 24.

113 ***The Key Underwood Coon Dog Memorial Graveyard:*** https://www.coondogcemetery.com.

115 ***Home cremation is carried out by a mobile cremation company:*** Louise Hung, "Build a Temple for Your Cat: Post-Death Pet Care in Japan," catster.com, February 4, 2015, https://www.catster.com/lifestyle/pet-cat-death-memorials-build-a-temple-japan-pictures-photos.

115 ***At its base there is a statue of a Buddhist saint:*** Hung, "Build a Temple for Your Cat."

115 ***More than 20,000 animal companions have been laid to rest:*** Erin Blakemore, "Commune with Pets of the Past at These Five Pet Cemeteries," *Smithsonian Magazine*, October 30, 2015, https://www.smithsonianmag.com/travel/commune-pets-past-these-five-pet-cemeteries-180957094.

115   *In the majority of cases, the pet:* Hung, "Build a Temple for Your Cat," updated June 24, 2015, by Vicky Walker.

116   *This is because Japanese people want their pets:* Hung.

119   *There are alternatives, which can be found:* "Jewish Resources for Mourning a Dog," accessed August 10, 2023, http://aftergadget.wordpress.com/grief-resources/jewish-resources-for-mourning-a-dog-with-inclusive-mourners-kaddish; "Pet Euthanasia and Memorials," officiant.org, accessed August 10, 2023, https://www.officiant.org/pet-funeral; Rabbi Susan Schein, "Burial Service for an Animal Companion," ritualwell.org, accessed August 10, 2023, https://ritualwell.org/ritual/burial-service-animal-companion; also Rabbi Joshua Snyder, "Creating a Ritual for the Loss of a Companion Animal," ritualwell.org, accessed August 10, 2023, https://ritualwell.org/ritual/creating-ritual-loss-companion-animal.

125   *These objects can lower cortisol levels:* Josee Ng, "Transitional Objects May Help with Grief Processing," glam.org, February 9, 2023, https://www.glam.com/1194443/transitional-objects-may-help-with-grief-processing.

127   *"'Keeping plush replicas of deceased pets helps the bereaved'":* Ng, "Transitional Objects May Help with Grief Processing."

128   *Others prefer to keep these precious items in a special box.:* For suggestions concerning the cutting, preparation, and care of pet hair/fur, see Mary Ruth, "How to Clip Your Pet's Fur for a Pet Hair Keepsake," tinypetmemories.com, September 3, 2017, http://www.tinypetmemories.com/articles/prepare/articles/prepare/keep-pet-mementos/a/how-to-clip-your-pets-fur-make-pet-hair-keepsake.

Heartbeat

131   *His name means 'eight':* Wendy Holden, *Haatchi & Little B* (London: Corgi Books/Transworld Publishers, 2014), 16.

131 ***Hatchi plus* kō *may mean 'prince':*** Holden, *Haatchi & Little B,* 16.

132 ***His story has been told in several films and books:*** A particularly beautiful picture book is Pamela S. Turner, *Hachiko: The True Story of a Loyal Dog* (Boston: Sandpiper/Houghton Mifflin Harcourt, 2004).

133 ***Sometimes Japanese parents are given a small state of an Akita:*** "Akita Dog Breed: Information and Personality Traits," hillspet.com, accessed August 10, 2023, https://www.hillspet.com/dog-care/dog-breeds/akita.

Chapter 5

136 ***"What we once enjoyed and deeply loved'":*** Helen Keller, *We Bereaved* (New York: Leslie Fulenwider, 1929), 2.

145 ***David Kessler, an expert on the subject of grief:*** Kessler, *Finding Meaning.*

153 ***He pronounced these inspiring words:*** Humans of New York, accessed August 10, 2023, https://www.humansofnewyork.com/post/43835301885/when-my-husband-was-dying-i-said-moe-how-am-i.

Conclusion

155 ***"There is nothing more whole than a broken heart."":*** This quotation has also been attributed to Rebbe Nachman of Breslov (1772–1810).

156 ***"The only whole heart is a broken one because it lets the light in."":*** See "David Wolpe, Judaism," *Lex Fridman Podcast* #270, November 28, 2022, https://podcastdisclosed.com/david-wolpe-judaism-lex-fridman-podcast-270.

157 ***"Listen to your heart, because 'only the heart knows'":*** Fyodor Dostoyevsky, *The Brothers Karamazov.* In my edition, translated

by David McDuff, "heart" has been translated as "soul": "only your soul is capable of seeking that which is precious" (London: Penguin, 1993, rev. ed. 2003), 376. I prefer Constance Garnett's translation of the word as "heart": "only the heart knows how to find what is precious." I accessed this translation online: Project Gutenburg, accessed August 10, 2023, http://gutenberg.net.au/ebooks07/0700061h.html.

157 *For he really lay buried in my heart:* Willie Morris, *My Dog Skip* (New York: Random House, 1995), 122.